GUIDED BY A TANGIBLE GOD

BY CHARLES SERIANNI

PREFACE

I wrote this book for a couple of different reasons. First, not knowing whether or not my work would be published, I simply wanted to chronicle my spiritual thoughts and experiences for my family and friends, as a reminder to them of how involved God truly is in an individual's life. When I refer to God, I am speaking of the triune God, the Father, Son (Jesus), and the Holy Spirit worshipped by Christians across the world. Secondly, in hope that my book would be published, I wrote it to reach people who doubt the existence of God and for people of other faiths who are seeking after the eternal. I also wrote this book for marginal Christians and sincere Christians alike who need to be inspired in their faith. I have witnessed over the years many Christians who seek after God but, for a variety of reasons, do not take the extra steps necessary to experience living in the supernatural where God is tangible for them.

I know from experience that the Creator of the Universe is

a tangible God.   I use the term "tangible" to describe a person's relationship with Him, and I need to qualify my use of this term. The basic definition of tangible is that which can be touched. The dictionary also informs us that anything that can be grasped, either with the hand or the mind is tangible. This is important, because many Christians like myself were taught as children that faith in God is a matter of believing without seeing, believing without any concrete evidence of His existence.   The fact of the matter is that for many Christians belief in God is not just a matter of faith, because they have experienced a tangible God. They have experienced the love of Jesus in a real way.

No, I do not claim to have seen God or physically touched Him. I do claim that I have physically felt God touch me, and I do claim that I have clearly heard Him speak to me. Furthermore, like millions of Christians throughout the modern world, I have experienced signs, wonders, and miracles that have provided me with the ability to grasp God in my mind. I am a Christian today, not by faith alone but through tangible experience and evidence.

I define myself as a Christian, not by membership in a denomination. Although for the past several years I have attended one particular Pentecostal church, I attend services where the Holy Spirit leads me based on the current situation and set of circumstances in my life. I, however, was raised Catholic, and I had a "born again" experience through the Catholic Charismatic Renewal in the early 1980's. During my tenure as a youth minister and my years of missionary service, I have worked and worshipped with people of all denominations. Consequently, I have great respect for the traditions of all denominations, and I feel comfortable in any liturgical setting where the presence of God is manifest. I find Jesus everywhere.

I also recognize that a certain lack of wisdom, poor judgment, and a misconstruing of God's word can be found in all denominations and individual churches, as well as in individual Christians. In fact, I am woefully aware of what my own shortcomings have been and continue to be. This is due to the human condition, the fallen nature of man. Rather than point the finger and pass theological judgment, I strive to accept the blessings, which each denomination and each Christian has to offer, and I pray that God's gentle correction eventually will reveal the truth to all of us.

I do not expect you to agree with all of my opinions expressed in this book. I am not trying to present theological arguments. My opinions have been formulated as a result of the signs and wonders and miracles my wife and I have experienced over the years in our attempt to live in accordance with the Will of God. Please view them in this perspective. The events and circumstances I recount on the following pages are as truthful and accurate as my memory allows. I have not embellished them. I merely ask that you give thoughtful consideration to what you read in a sincere attempt to examine your own spirituality and walk with God.

DEDICATION

I dedicate this book to my wife Donna whose spiritual

perseverance and faithfulness to God has kept me in

check when I easily could have gone astray.

GUIDED BY A TANGIBLE GOD

TABLE OF CONTENTS

CHAPTER ONE

THE CHALLENGE

WHAT DO YOU BELIEVE?

What do you believe about God? Whether you consider yourself to be a Christian or not, whether you attend church on a regular basis or not, whether you attempt to commune with God privately or not, what do you really believe and how did you formulate that belief?

The reason I ask is because the United States used to be a Christian nation. Our Founding Fathers were Christian and our heritage is Christian. Our sense of morality and decency, our entire value system was based on the fundamental principles delineated in the Holy Bible. The Preamble to our Declaration of Independence, for example, states:

"When in the course of human events, it becomes necessary for one people to dissolve the political bands which have connected them with another, and to assume among the powers of the earth, the separate and equal station to which the Laws of Nature and of Nature's God entitle them, a decent respect to the opinions of mankind requires that they should declare the causes which impel them to the separation. We hold these truths to be self-evident, that all men are created equal, that they are endowed by their Creator with certain unalienable rights…"

Simply stated, our Founding Father's believed the laws of "Nature's God" and the fact that "men are created equal [by God]" and "endowed by their Creator with certain unalienable rights," provide us the right to exist as a nation. This is a Christian belief that dominated our nation and culture until the nineteen fifties.

Unfortunately, a drastic and detrimental change has taken place in this great nation. We now live in a post-Christian era. Yet, the most current polls indicate that between 85% and 88% of U.S. citizens profess a belief in God. Of course, the poll results take into account people of all faiths and denominations. Yet, as an American citizen traveling in any country where another major religion is predominant, automatically, you would be labeled a Christian.

AN ORCHESTRATED EFFORT

I am concerned with our Christian heritage and what has happened to alter our beliefs as a nation. Secularism or the rejection of religion and all that it encompasses is the main culprit. Throughout the ages secularism and spirituality have been at odds. At the present time secularism has gained the upper hand in our nation. It has infiltrated American life and greatly influenced societal beliefs, value, and mores in all areas and at all levels of our society. This is especially true in education whether it be our local school district to our most prestigious institutes of higher learning. Generally speaking, the more prestigious the university, the more secular it has become.

Proponents of secularism have accomplished this change gradually by twisting the beliefs and principles of all faiths for their own purposes.   As secular attitudes have grown in influence and popularity, Christianity, in recent times, has come under direct attack, more so than the other major religions. This attack is most virulent from the elitist left who are the power brokers behind Hollywood and the mainstream mass media. They have an objective to subvert the fundamental, Christian principles upon which our nation was created and replace them with their personal perceptions of what they want our nation to be, perceptions that change with the prevailing winds of secular thought.

Secularists have successfully cried, " freedom of speech" and "freedom of expression," to the extent that common decency has been overshadowed by every vile and vulgar expression man can contrive. Moreover, they cry, "separation of church and state," in an attempt to marginalize Christianity while they attempt to eradicate historical evidence that our founding Fathers were Christians who believed the rights of man flow directly from God.

Think about this for a moment. How can one logically claim that our predecessors believed in "separation of church and state" when our Founding Fathers wrote in the preamble of our Declaration of Independence that our "right" to exist as a nation comes from God? Yet modern secularists adamantly cling to this falsehood as they ridicule and despise the truth of scripture as utter nonsense, reject faith in God, and create "new age" philosophies to replace Him, who is the Creator of all things.

There is no doubt. It is clearly evident that an intentional and well-orchestrated effort to marginalize Christians and Godly principles has become the accepted norm for the mainstream media controlled by the secular left. The result is that the United States, over the past few decades, gradually has become deeply secularized to the extent that many people do not even realize how our spiritual outlook, as a nation, has changed.

Many people in power, for example, whether it be in politics, the media, or even the church, who claim to be Christians, are merely superficial Christians who embrace secularism more so than the biblical principles taught by Jesus Christ. Subsequently, they ignore the teachings of the most respected religious leaders and modern day prophets. Instead, they advocate values and life-styles that are truly anti-God and harmful for America as a nation.

With the assistance of a highly biased news media and entertainment empire, these same people create their own pulpit to propagate their own version of what they claim is the truth about God and individual spirituality. The result is that we are daily bombarded from many quarters with twisted rhetoric, the voice of convincing lies, and an array of glamorized immorality and vice being advocated as normal behavior.

PERVASIVE INFLUENCE

Liberal secularism is so pervasive, it has affected the church-at-large to a greater extent than most Christians are willing to admit. Many people in this present generation of American society have been raised without the benefit of religious training of any kind, because their parents had been drawn away from the church by the attractions of the world enhanced and promoted by secular philosophy. Since this new generation does not feel the need to join a church, many denominations struggle to keep their church doors open. Their declining membership means that the propagation of the faith also is declining. A vicious cycle has developed which contributes to more and more people not being touched by the gospel of Jesus Christ. The United States is now as much in need of evangelization as any overseas mission field.

APOSTACY IN THE CHURCH

Furthermore, liberal thinking has seeped through the walls of the church and swayed the leadership of many main-line denominations, as well as individual pastors, to interpret scripture with secular bias and to preach doctrines that are anathema to the teachings of Jesus Christ. Sadly, many Christian leaders today rely more on worldly conventions than the grace of God for their understanding of spiritual matters.

The concept of holiness, the belief that the church should be an institution set apart from the world, a "Royal Priesthood," dedicated to the Lord Jesus Christ, is rapidly declining or ignored all together by many church leaders and certainly not understood by nominal Christians. From a biblical perspective we can compare the present day church, as a whole, to the nation of Israel in the years following the Israelites release from the rule of Pharaoh.

Scripture tells us that as the years passed God's chosen people, a nation set aside by God, turned from relying on Him for wisdom and understanding. Since they had no king to rule them, each man did what he felt was right in his own heart. In other words, there was no set rule of law, no standards for a man to judge the morality of his actions other than how he felt. Consequently, the people began to worship false gods and develop a lifestyle similar to their pagan neighbors. Likewise, today it has become commonplace for individual pastors and evangelists to preach a distorted gospel formulated in accordance with worldly logic and their own personal preferences, rather than expound on the wisdom and guidance of scripture.

Secularization of America's churches has become so broad, in many church quarters the Bible is rejected as the inherent word of God, and the long-standing precepts of Christianity have been replaced by changing and supposedly enlightened points-of-view. Many Christians now believe in a God whose character and moral dictates are merely a matter of preference and personal ideology. In short, many Americans, both inside and out of the church, have either rejected a belief in God or recreated a God that is easy to believe in. The Bible, for these individuals, is considered fiction, and many scriptural mandates, the very ones Jesus said he came to fulfill, are either watered down or rejected outright. The teaching in Hebrews 4:12 that the Bible is the

"Living Word" of God has been rejected by secularized churches.

LED ASTRAY

So pervasive and influential has liberal secularism become that the general population has been lead astray. Many people do not realize the extent of what has transpired in the United States. Even people who attend church on a weekly basis and consider themselves Christians, through and through, fail to heed scripture's reproach to "not conform to the world" (Romans 12:2). This is truly troubling in the light of what polls taken at the time of this writing tell us. The majority of Americans believe in a God. But what God? Again I ask, what do you believe, and what is your belief based on?

The truth is that we have become a nation of "believers" who possess no real understanding of who God is, what holiness means, or what one's relationship with our Divine Heavenly Father should be. We profess a belief in the Divine but forsake truth and knowledge of the Divine for what our own sinful nature and an evil world recreate as truth and reality. Faith has become merely a point-of-view that changes with the prevailing winds of a secular society.

I am deeply saddened that so many people in our own nation, both in and out of the church, have little understanding of the fundamental principles of our Judeo-Christian heritage. It was the faith of our forefathers that formed the basis for the foundation of the United States. By turning away from the truth of scripture, people unwittingly have turned their backs on the principles of faith and the accompanying blessings that have served to make our nation great.

REVISIONISM

For the past few decades, in particular, historical revisionists have been at work attempting to erase the faith of Our Founding Fathers and the impact their faith has played in so many aspects of American life. The faith of our Founding Fathers systematically has been eradicated from the history of our nation. Our public schools and the text books used by revisionists have been a key avenue for accomplishing this nefarious end through the twisting of some facts and the intentional omission of others.

A number of years ago, for example I was discussing the up-coming national holiday, **Thanksgiving**, with my ninth grade students. They told me that they had been taught in middle school that the purpose of the first Thanksgiving in America was to thank the Indians for helping the pilgrims! Furthermore, when I asked these students what President Abraham Lincoln had to do with establishing **Thanksgiving** as a national holiday, they were clueless.

As I previously stated, what once was a Christian nation now has become a post-Christian nation. The result is that our country, generally speaking, has turned away from spiritual truth. The basic guiding, biblical principles which have served to foster righteousness, peace, and prosperity in our decision making as a nation are now being rejected under the guise of "separation of church and state." As individual Christians and churches become even more secularized, our belief system and life-style pull us, as individuals and as a nation, further and further away from God.

PLACING GOD FIRST

The blessings that would fill people with joy, inner peace and assurance are not received by millions of Americans, because they do not possess the wisdom to sincerely seek after God's will. Of course, this is equally true for us as a nation. Scripture tells us, "Seek ye first the Kingdom of God and His righteousness and all things will be added unto you"(Matthew 6:33-34). Unfortunately, it is accurate to say, most Christians do not give much thought to placing God first in their lives, because their lives are wrapped up in secular thoughts, desires, and pleasures. Being successful, attaining wealth and prestige, and acquiring the luxuries of life are more important concerns than seeking after God.

Placing God first in our lives requires an act of will to turn our back on the ways of the world, including self-indulgence and self-reliance. This is truly difficult to do when we live in a secular society that inundates us with material excess, bombards us with explicit sinfulness, and preaches intellectual self-reliance. The typical Christian is more the molded product of a secular world than the vessel molded by the hands of God.

SELF-RELIANCE OR PRIDE

One of the major roadblocks to understanding the true nature of God is the secular misconception that we are a self-reliant people and the masters of our own destinies. This is just another twist to the age-old sin of pride, the sin that caused Lucifer's fall from Heaven (Proverbs 16:18-19). This is especially true of people who are highly educated and/or successful in their field of endeavor. Education and success oftentimes give us a false sense of who we are and what control we actually have over our destiny. Whatever our status in life, most of us go from day to day trying to control our own destinies when, realistically speaking, we have no assurances of what tomorrow will bring. One sudden, unexpected event can end our life or change it drastically. This happens to people everyday.

I am reminded of a conversation I had with a colleague who was a professed atheist. He told me a story about how he was tossing around a golf ball in a high-rise apartment building, a dozen floors above the street below. He lost control of the ball, and it flew out through an opened patio door and fell over the side of the balcony. Realizing that the velocity with which the ball was falling could kill a pedestrian below, he admitted that he exclaimed, instinctively, "God help me!" So much for controlling our own destiny! Fortunately for him, the golf ball did not do any significant damage.

I had a similar experience before I came into a personal relationship with the Lord. At the time I was involved in a general contracting and landscaping business. One of our wealthy clients had just completed the building of a million dollar plus home on a hillside overlooking a lake. My partner and I were standing near the house watching a couple of our crew at work. They were maneuvering a huge boulder into place on the hillside above the new house to create a natural yet decorative flavor to the landscape.

Much to our dismay, the crew lost control of the boulder, and it came rolling down the hill toward the house. We were paralyzed with shock. This mammoth piece of stone had to weigh a couple thousand pounds. Due to its weight and momentum, it had the potential of crashing through one side of the house and coming out the other.

Like my friend in the previous story, I instinctively sought out divine intervention by shouting out, "No, God!" I meant, of course, do not let this happen, God! This five foot high boulder rolled across the patio and rested up against the side of the house putting only a tinny, nick in the cedar clapboard siding.

The owner of the house had been watching the entire affair from his kitchen window. He was a real down-to-earth kind of guy who had worked his way up in the world from a farm boy in Vermont to a multi-millionaire developer. He calmly took it all in stride, no doubt, having had his own share of mishaps while constructing high rise buildings, shopping malls, and airports.

He succinctly expressed the spiritual reality of the situation by uttering an old adage familiar to most of us, "Someone up there must be watching out for you guys!"

Another truth, however, is that most of us go from day to day ignoring the wisdom of this adage, not caring about whether "someone up there" is watching over us. We play by our own rules and plot our own course, as we refuse to turn to God for advice or direction. Yet, His guiding Spirit often assists us during our times of need, even when we are not seeking His help. We fail to acknowledge that a loving God is watching over us. We prefer, instead, to indulge ourselves in the luxuries of the world to the point of ridiculousness and self-harm. Our appetites for all things of the world have become our priority. The Christian world now mirrors the secular world with the same cravings for wealth, luxury, pleasure, and ease of life. Our self-reliance, our pride, tells us that we deserve these things and we can acquire them without God.

HOW FOOLISH WE ARE

How foolish we are. When we open our eyes just a little bit and look around, how can we not help but see the result of pursuing the ways of the world rather than pursuing the will of God? Do we not see the multitude of individuals and families living in confusion and turmoil, afflicted by addictions of all kinds? Dishonesty, greed, hatred, anguish, insatiable desires, and misery on all economic levels of our society prevail. We may recognize the truth of what we see around us for a moment. We may even lament our condition temporarily, but we then rationalize the truth away or distort it to justify our current attitudes and behavior.

We seek wealth and status while the media headlines are replete with stories about the rich and famous who live ruined, unhappy lives. Divorce, dysfunctional children, drug addiction, alcoholism and dishonesty mar the lives of those we wish to emulate. Although we are aware of this, we turn our backs on the real cause of their misery. We watch the rich and famous squander their wealth and wallow in vice and addiction and, yet, we continue to strive after the very same things that have caused their wretchedness. Rather than seeking after God and His direction for our lives, we continue to pursue the desires of the world, which distance us from God and bring ruin to our own lives.

Attributes such as self-control, peace of mind, happiness and holiness elude us. Instead, we take pride in our intellectual prowess, but we do not have the fortitude or the conviction to deal with our problems or overcome our addictions. When problems confront us or a terrible tragedy befalls us, as self-reliant or successful as we thought we were, we fall apart emotionally and turn to alcohol and drugs for comfort.

Many people cannot even face the natural aging process without trepidation. Instead of turning to God and rejoicing in the gift of a spiritual life awaiting us after our physical deaths, we strive to stave off old age. We turn to the marvels of modern medicine where an array of "skin creams" and plastic surgery provide fleeting solace. How tragic is the fact that so many people stumble through the darkness of this world when the Light of the World, Jesus Christ, is readily available to guide their path (Psalm 119:105).

NOTHING HAS CHANGED

And yet, nothing has changed in the history of mankind.

As Ecclesiastes 1:9 states, "What has been will be again, what has been done will be done again; there is nothing new under the sun." The behavior of mankind we are witnessing today has taken place repeatedly throughout history. Every sin committed under the sun, every twisted belief and errant life-style conceived by man, every distortion of the truth, every desecration of the Divine, and even the outright rejection of Jesus, the Son of God, has taken place repeatedly, flowing endlessly from one generation to the next.

Isn't this why scripture relates and history verifies the destruction by God of entire cities and the decimation of powerful armies? When human wickedness was flaunted and rulers of nations took an unholy stand against the principles of God, He moved in righteous anger even unto the annihilation of the entire world by the Great Flood? Isn't this very same, persistent and ever present evil in the hearts of men the reason Jesus was rejected and crucified on the cross at Calvary?

Nothing under the sun has changed. Mankind, since the fall of Adam and Eve, lives under the influence of corruption and sin and is in need of salvation. That need is as urgent today as it has been at any time throughout history. Yet, rebellious men continue to deny the truth of God's word and reject salvation at every turn. They continue to live as if they are in control of their own destinies. In doing so, they create their own unhappiness and eventually destroy their lives in one fashion or another. Worse yet, they try to transform society, to get others to conform to their own corrupt and twisted mind-sets. The result is that the nation, the church, and the individual sow ungodliness and reap terrible consequences. They fail to heed the scripture that admonishes, "What good does it do to gain the whole world and lose your soul?" (Matthew 16:26).

WHAT IF...?

Of course, maybe there is no such thing as sin and evil. Maybe the Bible is just a mere collection of philosophical stories created by men to help make sense out of a world they were trying to understand. Many Christians, past and present have come to this conclusion about scripture and the **Old Testament** in particular. Maybe Jesus was just trying to make a point when He referred to himself as the "Second Adam" or when He stated that it would be worse for some sinners than it was for Sodom and Gomorrah (Matthew 10:15). Possibly, Jesus was psychologically misdirected when he proclaimed that He came to fulfill those scriptures that were really just a part of fictional stories. Possibly, He was just an irrational fanatic when He preached a gospel that He knew would lead Him to the cross on Calvary.

On the other hand, maybe all this is true. Maybe the Jesus whose teachings transformed western civilization was truly the Son of God. Maybe we need to understand what Jesus really taught. Maybe we need to adhere to the biblical principles that truly can transform our lives for the betterment of ourselves, our nation, and the world as a whole.

Again, I ask, what is your faith system based on? What is the teaching of your faith, your denomination or your individual church? Is it aligned with **Old Testament**

Scripture and the **New Testament** teachings of Jesus, or is it a washed out version of Christianity deeply influenced by secular thoughts and personal preference? You have to decide.

GROWING UP IN THE EARLY 1950'S

I grew up in a time and place where solid Judeo-Christian instruction and values held a strong bearing on the American family, a time when attending church was the normal thing to do and discussing spiritual matters was not a taboo. I recall with fondness the times during my childhood when I would walk with my grandmother to church. When we stepped outside on a Sunday morning, we had the pleasure of greeting many of our neighbors who also were walking to church. After many years of experiencing life and questioning my own belief system, I feel fortunate for having been raised as a Catholic during this era and having attended parochial schools where a basic faith, a sense of morality, and a reverence for God was instilled in me.

Like many other youth, however, I found church services to be boring compared to the temptations of a society that already was beginning to swing toward the secular point-of-view which today defines it. I strayed away from attending Sunday Mass and sought after a life of pleasure and excitement. Yet, even from my teenage years through my middle twenties when I served in the military and lived in the Caribbean, pursuing a lifestyle of self-indulgence, the spiritual knowledge presented to me as part of my childhood upbringing gripped my soul with deep and tenacious roots.

During my military years, I can recall standing on the fantail of a navy ship admiring the vastness of the ocean or standing on a Third World island at night looking up into the depth of the night sky ... and recognizing the work of God's hand.

I was awed by these special moments of enlightenment for what I recognized in my mind and soul as the immensity of God's creation and, yet, a mere reflection of His majesty. I can even recall experiencing a feeling of gratitude for what I was seeing and for the profound understanding it added to my life. At the time, I was not familiar with Psalm 8:3-5, but I knew it intuitively in my soul. It says:

When I consider your heavens, the work of your fingers, the moon and the stars, which you have set in place, what is man that you are mindful of him, the son of man that you care for him? You made him a little lower than the heavenly beings and crowned him with glory and honor.

Moreover, my early training later compelled me as a maturing man to live a moral life by restraining my indulgence in worldly pleasures. More importantly, whenever I did wrong, I did not attempt to delude myself. I recognized my sinfulness and experienced strong feelings of remorse.

During those times when I strayed the furthest from God and found myself in a difficult or fearful situation, my faith foundation served me well. I earnestly turned in prayer to my Heavenly Father. I admit there were many times when I treated God like the "Great Bellhop in the Sky," not the best attitude, for sure, but my Heavenly Father did not hold my prayers in disdain, nor did He punish me for my foolishness. Rather than ignoring me or chastising me for my indiscretions and sinfulness, He lovingly answered my prayers. He always reached out His hand and saved me from my circumstances. His mercy and unconditional love served to increase and strengthen my faith and, over the years, I was drawn gradually away from the wayward path of my youth.

OUR PRESENT SOCIETY

In today's world, unfortunately, too many people do not receive any kind of spiritual training in their childhood. Consequently, many individuals simply reject the concept of God outright or make no attempt to seek him out. Others who possess a rudimentary belief in God make no attempt to gain further knowledge of Him. For these people it is easier to shrug off spiritual values and moral dictates in favor of living the way the world proclaims one should live.

Even many church attending Christens are still spiritual babes-in-arms who are unwilling or find it too difficult to apply biblical principles to their lives. In Hebrews 5:11-14, St. Paul addressed this same issue in the early church:

We have much to say about this, but it is hard to make it clear to you because you no longer try to understand. In fact, though by this time you ought to be teachers, you need someone to teach you the elementary truths of God's word all over again. You need milk, not solid food! Anyone who lives on milk, being still an infant, is not acquainted with the teaching about righteousness. But solid food is for the mature, who by constant use have trained themselves to distinguish good from evil.

The fact is that the mass media has bombarded all of us so effectively with secular beliefs and attitudes that we have become spiritual babes-in-arms. We are either impervious to or unable to comprehend the sinfulness in our midst.

Shrouded in spiritual immaturity or blindness, many people who profess a belief in God refuse to grow spiritually. They ignore the power of daily prayer and the spiritual growth that comes from daily Bible study. They find every reason imaginable to rationalize away anything outside their comfort zone. When opportunities arise for them to draw closer to God or to receive his blessings, they scoff in their disbelief. Supported by the ideologies of the secular world, they turn away from God and reject his blessings.

For the longest time, in many ways, I was not any different. Into my late twenties I lived and functioned as an immature Christian. I believed in God, but since I was not actively seeking after Him, I only knocked on His door when desperate circumstances befell me. For the longest time, I never gave Him the opportunity to reveal Himself to me in a tangible way.

Although my fretful prayers were heard and I was extricated from the messes I had created for myself, I did harm and suffered harm. I lived in turmoil at times and missed out on many blessings. I just used the term "tangible," in reference to knowing and experiencing a relationship with

God. I have learned over the years that God actually touches us in a way that we can feel, sometimes even physically. If you are like the person I used to be, read the following chapters carefully. Seek spiritual understanding, as I give witness to how the Lord of All Creation is a tangible God whose presence will be made known to anyone who seeks after Him.

CHAPTER TWO

HIS SPIRIT POURED OUT

IN MY LATE TWENTIES

Fortunately for all of us, "nothing under the sun has changed," including God's love for us. Our omniscient and loving God has not abandoned us. In a continuous attempt to redeem his children, He has poured out His Spirit upon the world on numerous occasions. Historically, we have labeled these outpourings as reformations, revivals, and renewals.

One of these tremendous outpourings of God's Holy Spirit across the world occurred during my life. It became known as the Catholic Charismatic Renewal, and I became aware of it when I was in my late twenties. The Catholic Charismatic Renewal began with a retreat held in February 1967, by several faculty members and students from Duquesne University, a Catholic university in Pittsburgh,

Pennsylvania. As they prayed, they began to experience the manifestation of the Holy Spirit similar to what the Apostles of Jesus experienced on the day of Pentecost (Acts 2). Simultaneously, a group of students and faculty serving in campus ministry at the University of Notre Dame in South Bend, Indiana, began to experience spiritual signs and wonders. Unbeknown to one another, each group began to speak in tongues, to prophesy, to heal through the laying on of hands and to exhibit the "gifts of the spirit" as delineated in **Chapter 12 of 1 Corinthians.**

During this monumental time, the renewal spread like wildfire across the world. Many Catholic religious and lay people were drawn into a new relationship with Jesus, and entire parishes were renewed in response to this call of the Holy Spirit. Again, this was not a new development under the sun. God has poured out His Spirit innumerable times throughout the history of the world and the United States.

In accord with this particular spiritual revival, special gifts of the Holy Spirit flowed through thousands of Catholics just as they previously had flowed through Protestants during the Pentecostal Movement in our nation in the early nineteen hundreds. Numerous signs and wonders and miracles were manifested in a tangible way for those who were willing to step out in faith, even if reluctantly, to seek and to knock at God's door (Matthew 7:7).

Of course, history also repeated itself in a negative way, and many people both inside and out of the church scoffed at this new outpouring of the Holy Spirit. One of the biggest mistakes made by the Church in general was to view this event as a human movement, rather than as an outpouring of the Holy Spirit. Viewed from this perspective, the renewal was merely a man-induced phenomenon and could easily be rejected as emotional, spiritual fervor or even fanaticism.

Many Catholics refused to have anything to do with the Catholic Charismatic Renewal, and others vehemently opposed it as the work of the devil. When I first heard of these events I, too, was highly skeptical. I only attended my first charismatic prayer meeting to appease my wife who at the time was much more spiritually inclined than I was.

The pull of the world was great within me, and I was a "Doubting Thomas." As my wife Donna and I drove to our first prayer meeting, I prayed silently, "Lord, if this renewal is really of You, You will have to prove it to me." The meeting was being held at a private residence and led by a man whom I knew and did not particularly like. I reluctantly entered that house and challenged God to prove to me that the Renewal was real.

My challenge arose from my doubt, but my prayer was in earnest. God heard and accepted this prayer the way it was intended. Within minutes of the start of that prayer meeting, God responded to my challenge. The Holy Spirit came upon me, and I felt His presence in that private home in a way I had never felt Him during any church service I previously had attended.

It is difficult to put into words how I felt at the moment of my transformation. I felt an overwhelming sense of holiness, inner peace, and well-being. I knew without a doubt that God was not only real but also present in that room with us. Through the barrier of my own skepticism and my distaste for the prayer group leader, God made Himself known to me in a tangible way! I simply felt His presence. The proof that what I experienced was more than just an emotional reaction is found in the radical and lasting effect it had on me.

A CHANGED LIFE

My encounter with God at that prayer meeting changed my whole life in an instant. I was truly renewed in my faith and in my spirit. Later, as I studied scripture, grew in faith, and read about the Charismatic Renewal, I learned that what had transpired that evening was what Jesus meant when he told Nicodemus that he must be Born Again (John 3:3). It had nothing to do with water baptism or being a member of a particular denomination or even being saved. It was about a new awareness and commitment to God. It was about being empowered by the Holy Spirit, just as the Apostles had been in the upper room on the day of Pentecost when the Holy Spirit came upon them in the form of "tongues of fire" (Acts 2:2-4).

Of course, this encounter with God also was about turning away from my worldly way of thinking and acting. It required me to turn my life completely over to God and to acknowledge to myself that I needed Him to direct every aspect of my existence. Have you heard the expression, "Let go and let God?" That is exactly what I did and what so many intellectual and self-reliant people find too difficult a step to take. Over the years, I have had more than one person tell me that he needs to feel in control of his own life. These people, invariably, are still leading misguided lives and buying into many fallacious idea and errant faith systems created by the secular world.

In a short period of time after I turned control of my life over to the guidance of the Holy Spirit, I was so transformed, I began following spiritual paths that lead me to became a prayer group leader, a youth minister, a religious education teacher for teens, and a missionary. As I pursued these new paths God had laid out for me, my wife and I attended two world congresses on the Holy Spirit, numerous religious conventions, youth rallies, and healing services. I do not tell you this to brag, but to illustrate what it means to "seek and knock" in earnest.

As I pursued God and His Will for my life, I came in contact with Christian people of all denominations who were experiencing a life full of tangible signs, wonders, and miracles. The broader my experience in the Christian world became, the more I realized that everything we read about in scripture, the **Old Testament** stories and the **New Testament** proclamation that the "Kingdom of Heaven is at hand," were true. I quickly learned that we do not have to wait until we die to experience God's Kingdom. It is here with us and within us. And it is tangible!

A TANGIBLE GOD

Before I continue, allow me to clarify something. I do not wish to be theologically inaccurate. Scripture teaches us that it is better to believe without seeing; that is, to have faith in an invisible and intangible God (John 20:29). This is, without a doubt, the sacred ideal, a basic principle of holiness. Yet, Jesus did not immediately hold his own Apostles or the people to whom He preached to this strict dictate. In fact, this kind of faith is something that most of us have to spiritually grow into.

Hebrews 5:2 tells us: "He is able to deal gently with those who are ignorant and are going astray, since he himself is subject to weakness." In other words, since Jesus lived in the flesh as a man, he was subject to the same pain and suffering and the same doubts and temptations that we all experience. He, therefore, understands the reasons behind our disbelief. Scripture clearly shows us that Jesus answered prayers and direct requests in a tangible way. He performed miracles and provided signs and wonders that the people of his day could see and touch and believe. He did this out of compassion and love, but He also did this to encourage their faith and to provide tangible evidence of his divinity.

This was especially true for His apostles. In scripture we see the Lord's twelve men, a select group, exhibit a lack of understanding, doubt, and fear over and over again. They, too, just like us, were influenced by the secular and disbelieving world in which they lived. Jesus knew that the weakness of their flesh, the pull of a corrupt and secular world, and the influence of the Evil One would prevent His chosen apostles from developing a strong faith without some form of tangible evidence of the Divine. This always has been true for mankind in general.

I am a Christian who remains steadfast in my faith today, first, because it was ingrained in me as a child, secondly, because I was touched by the hand of God at that first prayer meeting my wife and I attended and, thirdly, because I have experienced a multitude of tangible signs and wonders during my life. Now, when times of doubt and despair begin to creep into my life, as they do all of us, I can believe without seeing for the moment, because God already has revealed Himself to me. The sacred ideal, the holy principle of faith, has been planted in my heart and soul and strengthened by tangible evidence of God's existence. I have been a firsthand witness of God's power and glory repeatedly throughout my life and, now, I am sustained in my faith.

EXPERIENCING GOD

One example of God's tangible manifestation that comes to mind occurred back in the1980's while my wife and I attended Mass during a charismatic conference at a Catholic university in Pennsylvania. The priest held up the monstrance, the vessel containing the consecrated host, the Eucharist, and simultaneously the entire congregation was literally "forced to its knees" in veneration. The power and glory of God's presence was immense and overwhelming at that moment. Just as St. Paul was knocked off his horse (Acts 9:3-4), all of us in attendance at that moment were overcome by the Divine Presence of God and literally forced down on our knees in adoration.

We all understood, instantaneously, that we were on Holy Ground in the presence of His Majesty, the King of Kings and Lord of Lords. After an experience like this, my Christian faith is no longer based on that which is solely intangible and invisible; it is based on rock solid evidence of a God, a Heavenly Father, who reveals Himself in a variety of ways to those of us who earnestly seek after Him.

EARNESTLY SEEKING AFTER GOD

If you are one of the multitude who either has ignored God or has been drawn away from the spiritual reality of God through the influence of our secular society or the misguided teachings of a church that has recreated God in accordance with its own selective point-of-view, you may read this with skepticism. You will ask yourself what appears to be a logical question, "If this is true, why haven't I or others I know experienced signs and wonders and miracles?" You will ask, "Why hasn't God revealed Himself to me?"

The answer is found in the following simple question: Have you actively sought after God and asked him to reveal himself to you?

To actively seek after God means to do more than attend a weekly church service or to pray on occasion when the mood or need strikes you. It means to pray in earnest and to study scripture, the Living Word of God. It means to seek an understanding of who God truly is. It means to travel in Christian circles and to avail yourself of God's teachings and promptings by reading a variety of Christian literature, listening to Christian radio, and attending Christian conferences. Simply stated, it means putting some real time and effort into drawing close to God.

Seeking after God is a continuous, life-long pursuit. As you begin to discover the reality of God, you must allow the promptings of the Holy Spirit to lead you where He may, even if it is to a place at which the world scoffs or to places outside your own comfort zone, your individual church walls, or even your present denomination. On many occasions I have had to say emphatically to lay people, priests, and pastors alike, "I am a Christian first, and a member of a denomination second. I will go where the Holy Spirit leads me."

In short, the answer to your question is, if you have not done these things, you have not experienced the tangible presence of God in your life, because you have not immersed yourself in the situations where God actively moves.

One doesn't find God while pursuing the ways of the world or in emulating those who despise the scriptures. The Holy Spirit moves where He will and in mysterious ways. Keep in mind, however, in order to actively follow the promptings of the Holy Spirit you need to turn away from the secular life-style and the misguided teachings of some churches. Often times the movement of the Holy Spirit is ridiculed and rejected not only by the world but by well-intended Christians and church leaders who have a limited understanding of God's ways.

MEDJUGORJE

A good example of this is the experience my wife had visiting Medjugorje, Croatia, one of many Marian apparition sights throughout the centuries. The mother of Jesus, our Blessed Mother has been appearing in Medjugorje since 1981. Many books have been written and university studies have been done concerning the signs and wonders and miracles that have been witnessed by millions of people since her apparitions and messages to the world began.

Even secular newspapers and various television programs, such as **60 MINUTES** have reported the phenomena. If you have been rejecting a belief in God, or putting little effort into seeking after Him, you may not have heard of Medjugorje or the multitude of miracles that have been witnessed there. If you did hear about Medjugorje, maybe you simply turned your back and wrote it off as more spiritual nonsense or the Devil's work in the Catholic Church.

Yet, millions of people of all denominations and faiths from across the world have sought out the message of Medjugorje over the past thirty plus years. Of course, it is the message presented by Mary that is important: **Pray and draw close to Jesus.** Those who have made a pilgrimage to Medjugore have witnessed and been blessed by signs and wonders and miracle's to strengthen their faith. If these miraculous signs have been so numerous, they even attracted the attention of the secular press, why haven't you heard of Medjugorge or looked into it further?

The "seekers and knockers" who have gone to Medjugorje or who have accepted what they have heard or read about Medjugorje have been spiritually blessed.

Thousands upon thousands of people have been provided with tangible evidence of God's existence as a result of our Blessed Mother's appearance at this town located in the former country of Yugoslavia, as well as Her appearance at other apparition sites throughout history.

Yes, Mary, the Mother of Jesus, Our Blessed Mother, has been appearing and calling the world to repentance for centuries. Of course the world-at-large, many non-Catholic Christians, as well as many Catholics either scoff at this possibility or give the whole idea little credence. In fact, The Holy See, the central governing body of the Catholic Church does not require the faithful to a accept or believe in Marion apparitions. However, The Holy See has officially confirmed the apparitions at Guadeloupe Mexico, Lourdes France, and Fatima Portugal, just to name a few of the more famous apparition sights. These particular Marion apparitions even attracted the attention of Hollywood, which produced highly popular motion pictures about them.

Have you heard of these apparitions, seen the movies, or know any of the details concerning what transpired? If not, maybe you should do a little prayerful research. You may even come to an understanding that God does not necessarily function in accordance with myopic, denominational thinking.

This is of ultimate importance: People who have responded to Mary's call have experienced spiritual conversion that has drawn them into a deeper, more personal relationship with Jesus. You see, the basic yet profound message of Medjugorje presented by Mary is not a deeply theological pronouncement. It is simply to turn to her Son, to keep your eyes on Jesus rather than the world and to repent. And to pray. Not exactly a controversial concept for a Christian, is it?

My wife went to Medjugorje on two different occasions in the nineteen nineties. She personally witnessed a number of amazing and miraculous events. Yet, when she returned home and gave witness to what she had seen or presented workshops about what she had experienced, few people in our community were interested. For many people, including the clergy, it was easy to simply reject my wife's accounts as emotional nonsense. For others it was simply too much of an effort, too great an inconvenience for their daily routine or perceived responsibilities to attend a workshop and seek after God. Some people, I am sure, simply told themselves that they "had God in their lives" and did not need anything more. Many people, unfortunately, had no desire to seek after God.

On the other hand, others sought out God through my wife's workshops and personal witness. These individuals were eager to learn about the message of Medjugorje, because they desired to draw closer to God. They were true seekers who were not disappointed. They were provided with a new, powerful, life-changing revelation of God.

My purpose here is not to promote Marian apparitions, it is to provide examples of how God continuously manifests Himself in our modern world and how many people do not see Him, because they are blinded by the corruption of a secular world and their own self-interests. The result is that they remain in the dark, totally unaware of what is taking place around them spiritually. This is true, of course, for even church leaders who for a variety of reasons have become spiritually blind.

SPIRITUAL BLINDNESS

Over the years, I have encountered and struggled against spiritual blindness in my community, among my friends, and in my own family. One of the most disheartening struggles for me has been with the clergy of various denominations. As a youth minister in my own hometown and as a missionary in many Caribbean nations, I have received negative reactions from both Catholic priests and Protestant ministers, who indignantly told me that they had been in ministry for many years and if these spiritual manifestations of which I speak are real, surely they too would have encountered them.

How does one respond to this type of attitude and skepticism on the part of "men of the cloth?" I do not wish to judge or belittle them. However, for whatever reason among many possibilities, these individuals have limited their own exposure to what God is actively doing in the world today. Keep in mind that the Seduces and Pharisees, the religious leaders during Jesus' time on earth, likewise, could not see or understand the spiritual reality that was manifested before them.

GRENADA

I experienced an example of this spiritual blindness one summer while on a mission outreach. A particular Catholic missionary priest in the island nation of Grenada was actually offended to the point of anger by my very presence as a missionary. On this particular occasion many years ago, I was working on a mission outreach with a worldwide, non-denominational mission organization, **Youth With A Mission.** Two of my sons and I were in Grenada willing to help further the Kingdom of God in any way we could. I had previously been in contact with the Catholic Bishop of Grenada who had welcomed me with open arms. Through him I was aware that a particular parish near the YWAM mission base was extremely poor and struggling to maintain a church and school. The school property was visibly in need of much repair.

When I met with the parish priest, I offered to bring in a work crew to paint the school and do a variety of repairs at no cost to the parish. This pastor rejected my offer of help after I witnessed to him concerning my personal, spiritual experiences and about Medjugorje. He discounted everything I had said to him and castigated me as an individual. He was outraged by my presence and what I stood for. He questioned the validity of my experiences and denounced Medjugorje because of the purported signs and wonders.

Then he challenged my role as a missionary. He asked me how I could call myself a missionary when I only spent short periods of time out in the mission field. He told me that he was a true missionary who had spent thirty years struggling and suffering in God's fields, and God had never revealed Himself to him in a tangible manner! Therefore, none of the signs and wonders and miracles to which I had testified could possibly be true.

Once again, I do not wish to judge this man. Who knows what hardships he had endured and what burdens he had carried throughout his tenure as a priest and missionary? I do know, however, that the negative and evil influences of the world had caused him bitterness and spiritual blindness. He flatly rejected the assistance God had sent his way through me. Consequently, he, the school children, and the people of his parish missed out in a number of ways. Just think of what may have been accomplished both physically and spiritually in that parish had this priest humbled himself and allowed an empowered team of Christians to work and minister in his parish.

GOD CANNOT POSSIBLY EXIST

I also have encountered people who avow that God could not possibly exist, because if He did, He would not have allowed all the terrible events to happen throughout history. He would not, could not, simply stand by and watch the perpetration of atrocities throughout the world without being moved to action. Furthermore, often times the same individuals claim that **Old Testament** stories about a God who destroys entire cities or orders the armies of his chosen people to put to the sword every man, woman and child of an opposing people are ridiculous, because a loving God would not act in such a way. Furthermore, they ask how could a loving and merciful God destroy the entire world as He did with the Great Flood?

Think about this for a moment. Does there not seem to be a contradiction in this type of thinking. On one hand, these people think that if God exists He would be moved to act against atrocities in our world. Why then are biblical stories of God taking action against atrocious kingdoms, evil people, and a corrupt world-at-large so difficult to comprehend?

The truth is that God has given mankind both a free will and a set of laws and principles to live by. Furthermore, he continuously has raised up spiritual leaders and prophets throughout history who have warned us of the consequences of our disobedience and the need to repent of our sinful and evil behavior. Scripture also admonishes that "fear of the Lord is the beginning of wisdom" (Psalm 111:10). God, in fact, is regularly moved to anger, direct intervention, and punishment, but only after He has provided mankind every opportunity to repent and change.

History also records how in His mercy and love God has divinely intervened in the lives of a multitude of people and historical events. History is replete with events and personal testimonies of both famous and common people who have truthfully related their spiritual experiences of how God has provided, protected, healed and even changed the course of events. Once again, an individual who is making a sincere effort to seek after God would encounter these facts and testimonials through a normal course of reading and association with other Christians. Scripture specifically tells us to ask for and expect direct intervention from God.

Scripture also warns us of the daily consequences of sinful behavior. God intervenes to bless and protect, but He also intervenes to prevent and punish. However, in His mercy, He always forewarns and provides the opportunity for the individual or the nation to repent before a chastisement is afflicted. The world, for example, was forewarned through prophets and Marian apparitions concerning both world wars. Moreover, God has given us the means to avert disasters and chastisements. It is always mankind that either scoffs at God's messengers or outright ignores them. Atrocities abound and evil prevails, because we allow them to as a matter of our free will. We do as we please and ignore God's warnings. And God always responds accordingly.

There should be no question about God intervening in this world. A quick Google search on line will provide you with sufficient reading for a lifetime on this subject. Secular history, as well as biblical history, provide numerous accounts of how mankind has brought doom and destruction upon itself. Our Heavenly Father is a loving God, but He is also a just God. He has given mankind a moral imperative to act against evil, and he has given us the spiritual means to do so. It is mankind, not God, who allows atrocities to be committed.

NOT BY FAITH ALONE

I am the Christian, the man of faith, I am today, because God is real and tangible. I do not have to rely on faith alone to believe in God. My eyes have seen tangible evidence of His existence over and over again. I have witnessed the direct intervention of God in my life and in the lives of others. Through my personal experience, I can testify to answered prayers and to signs and wonders and miracles. Without a doubt, I can proclaim that the greatest source of energy and power in the universe flows through prayer. Over the past thirty-five plus years, as I have brought every need and every circumstance before my Heavenly Father in the name of Jesus, my prayers have been answered in amazing ways.

My experiences and answered prayers are the result of actively seeking after God while living in an evil world against which we all must struggle on a daily basis. Quite often, however, our worst struggle is against our inner-self, which has been adversely influenced and weakened by a secular and evil world. While we seek after God, we must continuously pray for the grace to turn away from our own self-indulgence and self-deception, as well as the deception of the world. Furthermore, we must not allow our pride to delude us into believing that we are self-reliant and do not need God in our lives.

CHAPTER THREE

THE DIFFERENCE

The main difference between other people and Christians like myself is that peace and joy remain with us through all the circumstances of our lives, both good and bad. Do misfortunes befall us? Do I personally become discouraged at times? Of course, but God is ever-present, providing many blessings, averting dangers, and helping to carry my burdens. When afflicted with a problem or illness, no matter how severe, I have never prayed or been prayed over by others without being lifted out of my worries or despair.

Miracles literally have abounded in my life as a direct answer to the needs for which I have prayed. As you read through this next couple of chapters, I know you will be astounded by my testimony concerning how God has answered my prayers. I not only know a merciful and loving God who forgives me all of my transgressions, I have a Heavenly Father who numbers the hairs on my head, a Holy

Spirit who dwells within me, and a Savior who poured out His blood for me. I know an invisible God who consistently reveals himself to me through tangible evidence of his existence and love for me.

Most significantly of all, I have the assurance that Jesus Christ, through his death on the cross, has gained for me an eternal salvation. I have no fear of growing old, of death, or damnation, because I am a son of the living God (Romans 9:26) whose manifest presence and assistance is revealed to me daily. Through my faith, I have learned to redirect my thinking from a focus on what may or may not be possible in the natural to the supernatural where all things are possible (Matthew 19:26).

It is these tangible signs and wonders and miracles, which my wife and I have personally experienced, that I wish to share with you. I hope and pray that your heart will be touched, and that you will be drawn closer to God as a result of my witness on the following pages, no matter where you may be spiritually at the moment. Just keep in mind that my relationship with God is not unique. It has been the norm for millions of God's children throughout the centuries.

ANOTHER QUESTION

How many actual, incontrovertible, physical healings have you personally seen or experienced? Where does such a phenomenon fall into your faith-belief system? If you have never been healed miraculously or been present to witness someone else's miraculous healing, ask yourself why not?

The New Testament is full of accounts of Jesus and His apostles laying their hands on people or even simply speaking a word of healing and having it take place. Are these just contrived stories to propagandize the reader of the Bible into accepting a false belief system, or are these real-life accounts of what transpired over two thousand years ago? If they are real accounts, and I firmly belief they are, shouldn't we, as followers of Jesus, expect to witness them in our lives today?

BIBLICAL EVENTS RECUR DAILY

I contend that the Bible is the inherent word of God, that everything we read in it is true, and that the same events, the same signs and wonders recorded in the past are still taking place today, including miraculous healings. In fact, my wife and I have witnessed or personally experienced so many physical healings, I find selecting and placing them in a logical order for this chapter a daunting task. As you read these accounts of what we have personally experienced or witnessed, you will understand why our faith has remained so strong throughout the years. Our faith is in a loving God who continuously reveals Himself to us and answers our prayers.

HERNIA SURGERY

I will begin with the story concerning the events surrounding my surgery for a double hernia, because they took place shortly after I had had my "born again" experience. At that time, to supplement my income as a teacher, I was involved in a partnership with a colleague and close friend, doing all types of general contracting and landscaping. We had one particular client for whom we were doing extensive stonework. We constructed stonewalls and stairs winding up and around his new house built on a hillside overlooking Lake George in upstate New York.

We also constructed stone patios and rolled huge boulders into strategically selected locations to make a "landscaping statement" of natural wonder and beauty for wealthy clients. This work took place over a period of a few years. Being young and foolhardy, I bulled my way through this work recklessly straining my muscles to lift and move tons of stone. The end result was a double hernia that required surgery.

Trusting in the Lord to watch over me, I had no fear of having surgery. My wife and I simply prayed that God would direct the mind and hand of our doctor. For some reason, I reacted badly to the anesthetic and the surgery. I had difficulty coming out from under the influence of the anesthetic and, when I did, I felt and looked miserable. I was also in terrible pain. When my partner came to visit me shortly after my surgery, I looked so bad, he was frightened into giving up working with stone. My doctor and the nurses kept telling me that I needed to get up, move around, and use the bathroom. I wanted to comply, but the smallest movement on my part induced excruciating pain.

After several efforts to move of my own accord, I finally came to my senses, I lay back, and prayed for divine assistance. When I next attempted to get out of my bed, I was pain free and able to use the bathroom. As the days passed, the best pain relief I had available was the power of prayer. The healing process was slow and challenging, and it took me close to two months to completely heal from this surgery. Yet, whenever I was afflicted with severe pain I found immediate relief in prayer.

Why didn't the Lord heal me more quickly? I do not know. There are many possible reasons. What I do know is that He did not abandon me. He was at my side whenever I needed Him to help me carry this particular cross. When I did heal, it was a permanent healing in spite of warnings from my doctor and dire prognoses from others who had experienced the same type of hernia that it could recur. I have been trouble free for over thirty-five years, and have led a very physically active life.

THE SPOKEN WORD

Just a couple of years following my hernia surgery, I had a related experience concerning another double hernia that lead me deeper into the realm of the supernatural. This time it was my youngest son Nick who had the hernia. He was around two years old, and his hernia was congenital. My wife had taken him to Burlington, Vermont, for surgery, and I had stayed home in Ticonderoga to care for our other two sons. The memory of the long-time suffering I had previously endured from my hernia surgery weighted heavily on my mind throughout the day. The idea of my little boy being afflicted the way I had been was disturbing to me.

That evening following Nick's surgery, I was sitting by myself in the living room of our house after my other two boys had gone to bed. I foolishly gave in to my emotions, imagining the pain little Nick must be suffering. I actually began to fret nervously over his well-being. When I gained control of myself, I sought out the Lord in earnest prayer. As I prayed, I heard a voice in my mind clearly speak to me saying, "Open your Bible." Without a moment's hesitation, I reached down for my Bible lying on a side table next to my chair. I randomly opened this "Living Word of God" and read the first passage of scripture upon which my eyes had fallen. It said, "...and from this moment the child was healed" (Matthew. 17:18).

As I read this scripture a wall of apprehension crumbed from my mind and heart. An inexplicable sense of comfort and serenity flowed through me. Instantly, I knew that Nick was fine. I felt light-hearted and worry free, and I was able to go to bed and sleep peacefully. My wife returned home with Nick the following day, and he was already up and about. Our only concern then was keeping him from being too active too soon. He healed quickly and did not experience the pain and discomfort I had.

Even today as I recall what transpired that evening, I am in awe. A real, tangible miracle took place. I am not referring to the peace I felt or even the quick healing of Nick. I am referring to how God revealed himself to me in a way where there could be no room for doubt. Even today I cannot delude myself by thinking, it was only my own thought I heard and not the voice of God. You understand, of course, if it were only my own thought, if it were only I speaking inwardly to myself, how did I randomly direct myself to such a specific and meaningful scripture? By the way, as you shall see, this was not the only time I clearly heard God speak to me.

A RELUCTANT RESPONSE TO GOD

Over the years, as a youth pastor and a prayer group leader, I attended many youth rallies, and church services where both clergy and lay people with healing ministries were present. I also organized healing services for my own church and, on occasions, assisted in the laying on of hands and praying over individuals to be healed. I have witnessed people being healed as I prayed over them, but I never felt that I had a healing ministry. Instead, I always felt that I was merely doing what the Lord was calling me to do at that particular moment in time.

What transpired in my life, as well as my wife's, over the years was merely the spiritual result of actively responding to God as He called on us. As I allowed God to direct my activities, I was led into some amazing situations. Sometimes, I must admit, I obeyed reluctantly. Yet, the tangible healing power of God that I witnessed over the years so strengthened me in my faith, that when I later faced a horrendous accident and needed a personal, healing miracle, I did not hesitate to call in confidence upon the Lord.

My first hands-on experience with healing came unexpectedly. I am speaking of the very first time God called on me to lay hands on another person during a religious service and pray for a miraculous healing.

My wife and I were in attendance with my youth group at a Catholic Charismatic youth rally in a Catholic high school in Watertown, New York. With the assistance of my wife, Donna, and several parent chaperons, we had brought a group of over fifty teens to attend the weekend rally. We actually attended this rally for five consecutive years. The largest group we took consisted of eighty-six teens. We stayed with them in a motel each year, and we never had a problem with bad behavior. This was a miracle in itself. Our fundraising always resulted in sufficient funds to pay our expenses, and everyone who participated with us, both young and old, was blessed in many and varied ways.

On this first occasion I was seated in the auditorium while a Mass and a healing service were in progress. A Catholic priest, Monsignor Noel Zimmerman, and a laywoman named Jeanine Nichols were praying over the teenagers as they came forward. Jeanine Nicholas was a truly special person anointed of God with a healing ministry. She was a survivor of a Nazi concentration camp who at the time carried documentation from the bishop of our diocese stating that her ministry was authentic. As the years passed, I was blessed to get to know this woman personally and to assist her during several healing services.

At this particular moment, throngs of young people were going forward for prayer. Long lines of young people had formed before the prayer team, and it appeared to be an over-whelming situation for Jeanine Nichols and Monsignor Zimmerman.

I heard a voice audibly say to me, "Go down there and

help." I use the term audibly, because, what I heard was external, not in my mind. I actually looked around to see who had spoken to me, but no one was trying to get my attention. Recognizing that Jeanine needed help, I convinced myself that what I heard were merely my own thoughts. Besides, I had never participated in a healing service before, and I did not feel comfortable to do so at that time.

SLAPPED BY GOD

I remained seated in prayer, and a few minutes later I heard the same audible voice telling me to go down and help. Being in doubt about what I was hearing, I ignored the second request. I did not ignore the third order, because it was a vocal command accompanied by a hard, physical slap to the back of my head. The sting of the blow roused me instantaneously to my feet. I grabbed my wife and a couple other chaperons, and we went forward as a prayer team.

There were so many teens requesting prayer that the moment we established ourselves in the front of the auditorium, a massive line formed in front of us. Without realizing what was taking place, we found ourselves praying over five or six young people at a time. As they came forward, they formed a semi-circle around me with my prayer team members standing behind me. Each teen extended his arm forward to the center where they could touch each other's hands. As I reached out and touched their joined hands in prayer, they simultaneously fell backwards on the floor, "resting in the spirit".

If you are not familiar with this spiritual phenomenon, simply explained, the Holy Spirit of God comes upon an individual in such a way that his senses are overwhelmed, and he physically and mentally surrenders himself to God. The individual is not unconscious, but he is filled with an over-powering feeling of God's presence. He rests in this state while the Holy Spirit provides solace and healing.

I had witnessed this phenomenon happening while Jeanine Nichols and Monsignor Zimmerman were praying over the young people. I was not prepared, however, for it to happen when I prayed. To say that I was amazed is an understatement. I was experiencing this miraculous event firsthand, and I knew that I was not hypnotizing or pushing anyone down. All I was doing was praying and acting as a conduit for God's power. The following day numerous teens stepped forward following the Mass to give testimony to what healings they had experienced. I will not mention them here, because I do not have firsthand knowledge of what transpired following these testimonies.

The experience I had on this occasion, I later learned, was similar to what happened to Samuel in The Old Testament (1 Samuel 3:1-20). In this story about Samuel, who became a powerful prophet of God, he was not slapped by God, but he was called three times before he realized that it was God speaking to him. Once Samuel responded appropriately, scripture tells us that the Lord was able to use him to the extent that people recognized him as a prophet. I do not claim that I became a prophet on the level of Samuel, but from that first time I laid hands on people and prayed over them, my ministry with youth, the adult prayer group, and the church, as a whole, grew in stature and spiritual power.

A DOUBTING THOMAS

To illustrate how life changing this experience was for me, allow me to digress from my narrative for a moment to describe my first encountered with the blessing referred to as "Resting in the Spirit." From the first charismatic prayer meeting I attended after having my "born again" experience, I repeatedly witnessed individuals resting in the Spirit. Yet, like the Apostle Thomas, I was having my doubts about what I was seeing. I had never experienced this phenomenon, even though I had been prayed over several times. I guess I was chalking it all up to emotionalism.

A few months after my first prayer meeting, I attended another prayer meeting where only five other people, all older women, and the prayer leader were in attendance. At the end of the meeting, the prayer group leader prayed over each woman. One after another, they rested in the Spirit. I tried to focus on praying along with the others but, instead, I was thinking to myself, what nonsense! These are just a bunch of emotional women.

Once everyone but I had been prayed over, the group turned to me and kindly insisted that I be prayed over, too. I was too embarrassed to refuse, so I allowed them to lay hands on me and pray. I stood there and, once again, as I had been prone to do in the past, I challenged God, "If this is real, Lord, You have to prove it to me." I no sooner had expressed this thought in my mind, than I became aware that I was on the floor after having been under the influence of the Holy Spirit for several minutes.

I cannot find words to express the sense of peace and joy that consumed me as a result of being tangibly touched by God in this special way. Keep in mind that I did not deserve this blessing after I had challenged God in such an audacious manner. You do not have to deserve God's miraculous touch either. All you have to do is seek after Him and step out in faith by placing yourself in situations where the Holy Spirit is moving. I did this by attending that prayer meeting and by reluctantly allowing the group to pray over me.

When I took part in the healing service at that particular charismatic youth rally in Watertown, I was actively trying to follow a call on my life to be a youth minister and bring young people into a personal relationship with Jesus. I was where the Holy Spirit was moving. Little did I know that the Lord would touch me in such a dramatic way as a slap on the back of my head.

A voice one hears can be explained away, but a physical slap that inflicts pain and startles you cannot be so easily discounted. From that day forward, I did not hesitate to lay hands on people, whether they were adults at our prayer meeting or teenagers attending my youth group and religious education classes. In subsequent years, I fostered healing services by assisting others in their ministry and by organizing such services in our own church. Yet, as I previously mentioned, I never felt as if I possessed the spiritual gift of healing.

ASTOUNDED IN RELIGIOUS ED. CLASS

Over the years I heard many testimonies from people who had been healed at one of the services in which I participated. Since I have no way of verifying them, I will limit my narrative only to those circumstances in which I personally can give testimony and to a few experiences related to me by individuals who were very close to me and whose veracity was unquestionable at that time.

One of the most amazing situations I encountered occurred in one of my religious education classes. I was teaching about the charismatic gifts mentioned in scripture (1Corinthians: 12), and I started discussing with my students healing through the laying on of hands.

One of my high school students, a real wise guy, openly scoffed at what I said. He had sprained his ankle at soccer practice just before coming to my class. He was in pain, and he was limping when he got out of his seat and came forward. He actually challenged me to lay hands on him and pray for a healing. Keep in mind that I never felt as if I had a specific gift of healing, but at that moment I was so emboldened by the Holy Spirit, I did something I typically would not do. I proclaimed in confidence to my class that this student would be healed.

As he stood in front of me before the class, I reached out my hand toward him and began to pray. I did not touch him, yet a spiritual force flowed from me that did. He was knocked backward about three feet. He banged against a sidewall of the classroom and slid down to the floor.

Neither my student nor I had expected this astounding result to my prayer. His eyes, like mine, were as wide as saucers as he sat on the floor momentarily confused. It took both of us a few seconds to recover from our initial shock. The other students sat in an awed silence. Then the young man lifted up his leg and shook what had been his injured ankle. He slowly got to his feet and put his full weight on his ankle. The pain and the swelling were gone.

He was healed! At that moment there was no doubt in any of our minds that this teenage boy had been tangibly touched by God in a miraculous way.

This is the only time that I felt the Lord tell me to claim a healing in advance of praying for an individual. I presume that this took place, because a greater good was served beyond touching one disbelieving teenager with a healing. All of us present in that classroom had experienced the hand of God moving in an astonishing and tangible way. My faith, as well as the faith of all my students, was strengthened by this display of an omniscient and powerful God.

In the years to come, the majority of my religious education students came forward at one time or another for the laying on of hands during my religious education classes, prayer meetings, and other religious services. Many of my students and youth group members, in fact, developed the spiritual practice of praying and laying hands on one another. They even astonished a couple of our local priests and several of their own parents who "rested in the spirit" when these young people prayed over them.

CHAPTER FOUR
MAJOR HEALINGS

PRAYER WARRIORS

God's power is not necessarily an invisible power. For those individuals who actively seek Him out, His power frequently manifests itself with a tangible result, especially when intense, sincere prayer is involved. On one occasion, my oldest son Demian was "remodeling" his tree fort on the wooded edge of our backyard. He was about twelve years old at the time. My wife and I were in our living room visiting with three former youth group members, three young women who now were students at the University of Steubenville, at the time a Catholic Charismatic University. They were back in town on a school break and had stopped by our home for a visit.

We heard Demian enter the house through the backdoor

that led into our kitchen. When we heard his muffled call for me, instinctively we knew there was a problem. I led the way into the kitchen, and found my son standing there with his hand covering his mouth. Through his blood streaked hand he mumbled, "I think I hurt myself."

When he removed his hand from his mouth to reveal the injury, I almost fainted at the sight of what I saw. A long two by four with a nail protruding through one end had fallen from where it had been leaning up against the wall in his tree fort. The nail hit him in the corner of his mouth and sliced downward in a semi-circular fashion cutting a three-inch long wound. With his hand removed, his lower lip flapped down to his chin.

Whenever I am injured, I can control my pain and fear. I typically remain calm and have the presence of mind to pray. When someone dear to me is injured, I panic. This has always been one of my weaknesses. I guess I am so concerned for my loved one's well-being, I am overwhelmed by what I perceive may be the person's pain and suffering.

Demian's injury truly upset me. Even though I started praying as I ushered him into our car for the drive to the emergency room, by the time I got to the hospital with him, I had gone into shock. While the doctor attended to Demian, I had to sit in the hallway and regain control of myself both mentally and physically. I prayed but received no comfort, because I was praying in the natural unable to truly turn the situation over to God.

My wife had remained at home with our two other

children and the young women from Steubenville. Fortunately, they had the presence of mind to go into deep intercessory prayer for Demian. By the time the doctor finished doing the stitching, Demian was relaxed and feeling pretty good. He looked a lot better, too, but the doctor warned us that he would have a nasty looking scar. During the following days, we prayed earnestly that Demian would heal quickly and that the scar would be minimal.

Ten days later the stitches were removed from Demian's chin to reveal a healed wound. In another week after the swelling had dissipated there was only the slightest indication of a scare below his bottom lip. Today one would have to search Demian's face carefully to find that scar. Once again, our prayers were answered by a loving God in a miraculous way. A Heavenly Father had taken control when an earthly father had panicked.

If the last two miraculous interventions by God to which I have given witness have not convinced you of how powerful prayer is, or how readily our Heavenly Father reaches out to those of us who seek after Him, maybe my next story will transform your disbelief. It involves an injury that will cause anyone to shudder at the thought of it. What I now narrate is a witness to one of the most amazing and miraculous healings I personally have encountered. I say this with all sincerity and veracity, because it happened to me, not someone else.

AN ENCOUNTER WITH A TABLE SAW

A couple of years before Demian's injury to his face

occurred, I experienced what could have been a devastating injury to my right hand. It happened on the afternoon of New Years Eve of that particular year. My wife had taken our two younger sons with her to Niagara Falls to care for her mother who was ill, while my oldest son Demian and I remained at home in Ticonderoga.

I was sitting in my recliner reading when Demian approached me and asked if he could use my table saw. It was set up in the basement of our house. He was working on a wooden car for cub scouts and wanted to make a small, decorative cut on it. Ironically, I lectured him about the dangers of using a table saw, and said I would make the cut for him.

The two of us went down into the basement, and I adjusted the blade at the correct height and turned on the saw. As I began the cut, the wooden car started to bind on the blade. Before I could react, the force of the blade kicked the piece of wood away, and I dropped my right hand on the spinning saw blade.

As I said in the previous story, when I am injured, I typically remain calm. However, there is more involved here than just my self-control. There have been times in my life when I strayed off on a tangent from my walk with the Lord, and times when I walked exceptionally close to Him. This was one of those periods, fortunately, when I was walking very close to Jesus.

My immediate, split second reaction was panic, and I was afraid to look at my hand. However, my fear passed instantaneously. The grace of God held my emotions in check and placed a prayer in my heart. Without looking at my right hand, I calmly reached over with my left hand and turned off the saw. And I prayed, "Lord, I give these fingers to you, but if it be your will, please save them for me."

GOD INTERVENS

The moment I recited that prayer, the most wonderful feeling of love and well-being flooded over me. My physical being was literally lifted into the supernatural realm where one experiences the presence and peace of God. No words were spoken to me, but I knew that I had nothing to fear. I knew that my fingers would be okay. I now looked at the devastation to my right hand and to the look of horror on the face of my son.

My little finger was sliced from the outside inward through the fingernail. My ring finger was sliced downward from the top to the bottom of the nail. My middle finger sustained even worse damage. It had been sliced downward from the tip of the finger to the second knuckle. The flesh on the right side of this finger was hanging by a thread.

I instructed Demian to go upstairs and get me some paper towels, which I used to wrap around my fingers and apply pressure. Calmly, we went outside, got into my car and started driving to the hospital emergency room. A short distance from our home, we saw our close friends, Jim and Linda, out for a walk. Since it was difficult to drive and keep pressure on my injured fingers to stem the bleeding at the same time, I pulled over and asked them to drive me the rest of the way.

Once we arrived at the hospital, I sat peacefully awaiting the arrival of the same doctor who later stitched up Demian's chin. When he examined my fingers, he told me grimly that he didn't think he could save my middle finger and that there would be nerve damage to my other fingers. I was floating in the supernatural, however, confident that God was in control. I don't know what must have gone through the doctor's mind when I nonchalantly shrugged off his prognosis and told him to stitch up my fingers the best he could.

I was so at peace with the situation, I felt no pain and experienced no immediate after effects. I felt so good, I attended a New Year's Eve party that evening and went jogging the following morning and every subsequent morning until the stitches were removed from my fingers ten days later. The doctor was amazed at how well my fingers had healed, but he warned me that I would not regain feeling or movement in my middle finger.

A week later when I returned for a check up, he was astonished that I had complete feeling and movement in all my fingers. He literally shook his head in wonder as he examined my hand. During this time of healing, I had experienced no pain whatsoever. By the way, my little finger and ring finger healed without any scarring or disfiguring of the nails. My middle finger, however, is visibly indented where the flesh had been cut away, but in the passing of over thirty-five years it has not been a problem for me.

CONFIRMATION OF THE MIRACLE

This story doesn't end here. Whether it was the devil trying to steal away my blessing or the Lord confirming the miracle I had received in such a way that no doubt could be attributed to it, I am not sure.

About six months after the initial injury, a large cartilaginous growth developed along my injured middle finger. When I returned to my doctor for treatment, he again expressed wonderment over the fact that I had feeling and movement in that particular finger. As I mentioned my middle finger is not only scarred, but a visible chunk of flesh is missing. Due to the severity of the original injury, my doctor advised me to go to a hand clinic in Burlington Vermont, to have the growth removed.

The specialist at the hand clinic in Burlington expressed the same amazement as my doctor had while he examined my finger. He told me that there was no physiological explanation as to how I could have feeling and movement in my middle finger, considering the amount of damage he was seeing. He further explained that the surgery to remove the growth was a delicate one. He forewarned me that this time I most likely would lose feeling and movement in that finger. I remained at peace about this and felt confident that God was still in control. Without a moment of hesitation, I asked the specialist to schedule me for surgery.

The surgery was successful, and despite the dire prognosis, I retained both feeling and movement in my middle finger. It is said that God works in mysterious ways, and in the case of my finger, God's mysterious handling of the situation became even more perplexing.

In the course of another six months, a second cartilaginous growth appeared on that damaged finger. By this time I was seeing a different family doctor, a woman who also happened to be an excellent surgeon. When she examined my finger for the first time, she, too, was astounded that I had normal function.

I explained to her that I did not want to go back to the hand clinic, because the doctor had made a big and expensive process out of performing the surgery. I asked her if she just could remove the growth in her office. She was hesitant to do so. She told me that the slightest slip of the scalpel would result in nerve damage. We had a good doctor-patient relationship, and I assured her that I would not hold her liable for any negative effects of the surgery.

My understanding of the way God was dealing with my finger was limited, but I still was confident that He was still in control. Against her better judgment, I was able to persuade her to perform the surgery, and she successfully removed the growth right there in her office. Since the third surgery over forty years ago, I have not had any problems with that finger.

Over a year and a half had passed from the time of my original accident with the table saw through my third surgery. During this time, I walked in total confidence that a loving Heavenly Father had intervened and blessed me with a tangible, miraculous healing to which three different doctors could not give a physiological explanation. Even with the two successive growths, I did not become discouraged or anxious. Quite the contrary, I was eager to witness to everyone how God was taking care of me.

My faith was strengthened as a result of this situation and, possibly, some people to whom I witnessed were also drawn closer to God. This is one reason why my wife, Donna, and I have remained steadfast in our faith. With each miraculous encounter we have with God, the cumulative evidence that He is neither distant nor intangible affirms our faith.

Do you still have doubts about miraculous healing? Place yourself in my shoes right now as I sit here typing this story with my healed fingers. Could you not but help to examine that middle finger, to feel the indentation and scar, and not be amazed as I still am?

AN EGG SIZE TUMOR

The next miraculous healing to which I give witness is truly remarkable when viewed from solely a natural perspective. It defies explanation unless you step into the supernatural. It occurred just a few years before my wife and I retired. My widowed mother was still living in our family home in Niagara Falls, New York. At that time, she was in her middle eighties and had been having problems with palpitation of her heart and dizziness. She was shopping in a grocery store one afternoon when her heart began to palpate wildly. She became dizzy and fainted while standing in the checkout line.

Rushed by ambulance to the nearest hospital emergency room, she underwent a series of tests including an MRI and chest x-rays. A heart specialist was called in, because the tests revealed an egg-size tumor in the right ventricle of her heart.

She was transferred to a special cardiac treatment center in Buffalo, New York, where the presence of the tumor was confirmed. My older brother, Richard, was a PhD, teaching physiology at the University of Pennsylvania. He met with my mother's doctor and reviewed all the test results and images of her heart. He, too, confirmed the existence of the egg-size tumor in her heart. The prognosis was not good. We were informed by the heart specialist that without surgery my mother would surely die. On the other hand, he told us, considering her age and other medical problems she had, her chances of surviving heart surgery were minimal.

RISK TAKING WITH GOD

After prayerful consideration, my mother decided to have the surgery. She was prepared to go home to the Lord should the surgery not be successful. Our prayers now shifted from seeking a healing to a successful surgery. On the morning of her surgery, as we sat in the waiting room praying, we were informed that my mother would be taken into the operating room shortly, and that the surgery would take several hours.

All my family members went to the cafeteria for coffee. I remained in the waiting room and kept a prayerful vigilance. Within forty-five minutes of my mother having been taken into the operating room, her surgeon came out looking for her family.

A BEWILDERED DOCTOR

Due to the brevity of time since my mother was taken into surgery, I assumed the worse had happened, that she had passed away on the operating table. Instead, I learned that our Lord's healing hand had been at work. What the surgeon explained to me caused me to shiver in amazement. He informed me that the standard procedure prior to surgery was to redo all of the tests. Incredulously, the new tests showed no sign of the tumor. Therefore, my mother's surgery had been canceled. The surgeon was bewildered by this new development, and he had no plausible explanation to offer.

Of course, we all were astounded by this inexplicable event. That is, inexplicable in the natural but not in the supernatural. Later on when I gave this miracle some further thought, I was awed by the way God had responded to our prayers. Remember, we had shifted from praying for my mother's healing to praying for her surviving the surgery. Yet, in His omniscience and benevolence our Lord had provided a total healing.

A few years later, when we retired, my mother moved to Florida with us and lived another three years. During this time she had the blessing of enjoying life with her younger sister, her great grandchildren and a number of friends who lived close to our retirement home. My mother was taken home to the Lord at the age of ninety. Once again, a Heavenly

Father touched our lives in a loving and tangible way. He provided my mother with an additional six years of life.

CHAPTER FIVE

THE CARS

BRING EVERY NEED BEFORE THE LORD

Most people of faith will pray for themselves, a loved one or a member of their church who is seriously ill or facing a desperate situation. The more dire the circumstance, the more likely it will elicit prayer from the typical Christian. Conversely, people of faith often do not pray for minor physical ailments, such as colds or stomach viruses. Similarly, one is less likely to consider more common, mundane, everyday needs worthy of prayer and divine intervention. Scripture tells us, however, to bring every need before the Lord who will give us all good things (Philippians 4:6).

Over the years I have prayed over cars with mechanical problems and home appliances that were malfunctioning. I can recall one particular blustery winter evening when a group of us came out of a spiritual conference in a distant city to find the driver's car unresponsive. Turning of the ignition key elicited only cold silence. We were pumped up high on praise and worship, and we did not hesitate, as a group, to lay hands on that car. When the driver subsequently tried the key, the engine roared. We returned home safely that evening without any further problems.

I frequently pray for parking places, quick lines at the checkout counters, and guidance when I am doing any type of skilled labor. If I am doing carpentry, I pray, "Lord, you were a carpenter in life. Please guide my eye and my hand." I have found the results to be phenomenal... no, miraculous. By the way, I have also learned never to buy a car or truck without praying first and waiting for God's perfect timing.

A RECURRING MIRACLE

The "miracle of the cars" began back in the late 1980's and has reoccurred on a regular basis for me up to the time of the writing of this book. As you will see, this story illustrates how God hears our prayers and responds with blessings that can overflow beyond our greatest expectations, no matter the need we bring before Him. I am still astonished by God's provision in this matter, and every time I go outside and get into my car or truck, I give Him praise and thanks.

As you know, for most of us, cars are a necessary and an expensive commodity. Many people incur significant monthly payments that stretch their budgets to the limits, so that they can own or lease the type of car they feel that they need or even deserve to maintain their standard of living. Other people simply purchase a car out of necessity, try to stay within their budget, but still find their finances being stretched and stressed by monthly payments.

My wife and I fall into the latter category. Due to limited finances since children blessed our marriage, we have always purchased used cars. We felt that the cost of buying a brand new car was beyond what we could afford. When raising a family and manipulating our budget to make ends meet, we did not need the stress of a hefty, monthly car payment. We may have been acting prudently in this matter but, at first, we were not functioning spiritually. For the longest time, unfortunately, we never considered the need to pray in earnest over the purchase of a car. Consequently, our choice of vehicles ended with mixed results, some good and some bad.

The "miracle of the cars" began with old friends of ours from Niagara Falls, New York, who gave us an entirely new perspective about praying for every need. Donna and I grew up, attended college, and married in Niagara Falls, New York, while I was still in college. During our college years, we had good friends by the name of Al and Maureen. They became engaged and were to be married the summer of 1968, following their graduation. When Donna and I accepted teaching positions in the U.S. Virgin Islands that year, Al and Maureen bought all of our furniture and planned to move into our vacated apartment once they were married.

Since our paths took different directions over the years,

our contact with Al and Maureen was minimal. We exchanged Christmas cards and met with them occasionally at a restaurant for a short luncheon whenever we were visiting relatives in Niagara Falls. In the middle eighties, after seventeen or so years had passed in this fashion, Al and Maureen contacted us. They let us now that they would be passing through Ticonderoga, New York, where we had made our permanent home until our retirement. They were planning to visit colleges in the Burlington, Vermont, area with their oldest daughter who would be graduating from high school at the end of that school year.

WITNESSING LEADS TO INSPIRATION

We were delighted at the prospect of seeing them, and we made arrangements for them to spend the evening with us on their way to Burlington, an hour and a half drive from our home. After dinner on the evening of their arrival, our conversation shifted from reminiscing about old times to our present life situations. By this time, my wife and I had had our "born again" experience, and we were heavily involved in various ministry work. I was a prayer group leader and a youth pastor in my own organization, **Teens for Christ**. Donna, likewise, had developed a ministry to the dying at our local nursing home where she was the director of social services.

Much to our surprise we learned that Al and Maureen, too, were heavily involved in their church as a result of their exposure to the **Catholic Charismatic Renewal**. We began sharing stories about the amazing and even miraculous events we had experienced over the years since giving our hearts to the Lord. One of the extraordinary stories Al and Maureen shared with us was about a miracle they experienced concerning the purchase of a car.

They, too, had been living on a limited income. Al was working as a nurse, and Maureen was a stay at home mom who worked as a substitute teacher to help make ends meet. They had a large family consisting of several children, the exact number I do not recall. Their old car had been on its last leg, and they started praying about buying a station wagon to accommodate their large family.

Back in those days, a station wagon was the big family car. This was the time before vans and SUV's became popular. The typical wagon had a third seat facing backward and could accommodate eight passengers. It was also the time before seatbelt laws were as stringent as they are today. On a long trip, a family could lower the third seat in the back of the wagon, throw down a sleeping bag and quilts along with some toys, and create a play area for a few of the younger kids. A station wagon was an ideal vehicle to accommodate a large family.

The only problem was that station wagons were expensive by the standards of that day. Brand new, full-size wagons, back in the eighties, were selling in the high teens to the low twenties. Even used wagons with low mileage were priced in the range of fifteen to seventeen thousand dollars.

After praying for several weeks, Al and Maureen started searching for a used station wagon. They felt that their financial circumstances would allow them to take out a car loan for no more than nine thousand dollars. Keep in mind that a typical yearly salary for nurses or teachers at this time was about fifteen or sixteen thousand dollars. When they explained what they were looking for and their limited price range to various car salesmen at different dealerships, they were actually laughed at. They were told, point blank, with no punches pulled, that they were out of their minds. There were no decent station wagons to be found in their price range.

Undeterred, they continued praying as a family for God's provision. In a matter of a couple of weeks, they received a call from a salesman at one of the dealerships they previously had visited. He informed them that an elderly man just had traded in a three year-old station wagon with only seventeen thousand miles on it. Condition wise, it was almost a brand new car. The dealership had not gone through the car to check it out mechanically or to clean it. The manager was willing to sell the car for nine thousand dollars, "as is," if Al and Maureen would purchase it immediately!

Al and Maureen considered this to be a miraculous answer to their prayers. Once they saw the car and took it for a test drive, they purchased it without reservation. The car, in fact, did turn out to be a real blessing as the body and interior were in excellent condition, and it proved to be mechanically sound.

WISE BUYING OR A MIRACLE

Donna and I immediately accepted the veracity of this story. It was one of many miraculous stories we were sharing concerning our own personal experiences while walking close to Jesus. A skeptic, on the other hand, would say this is a nice story, but there is nothing miraculous about it. He would logically conclude that certain specific factors were in play that lead to this great deal for Al and Maureen.

For instance, they had canvassed all the dealerships in their area indicating that they were ready to buy. They stuck to their price, were patient, and when the opportunity arose, they did not hesitate to buy. Financially speaking, isn't this what we all should do? Isn't this just sensible and shrewd buying that has lead to many people getting a great buy?

The skeptic is right on this point. Many people have gotten great buys through the use of common sense and patience. However, when God creates a miracle, He deals in the supernatural that confounds all human logic. Al and Maureen's experience is only the beginning of this miraculous story. There is much more to it. What happened to us after we heard this story is what truly confirms God's miraculous hand at work.

As I have said, by this time in our new spiritual walk with the Lord, I had established my own nondenominational youth ministry. My wife and I were constantly driving kids around to church services, Christian music concerts, weekend retreats, and a variety of other activities. Like Al and Maureen, we also needed to replace our car, and a station wagon sounded ideal. Our finances also were quite limited, and we would have to carry a loan to make a purchase. Just like Al and Maureen, we only could afford a loan in the $9000 range.

THE MIRACLE IS SHARED

Impressed by what Al and Maureen had told us, we started praying for our own station wagon. About five or six months later in the spring of the year, I felt God telling me it was time to start looking for another car. On a bright and sunny Saturday morning, I took my youngest son Nick along with me to shop for a car. He was seven or eight years old at the time and eager to spend the day with dad. We drove south down Route 22 from Ticonderoga toward Glens Falls, New York, the nearest, large city about an hour's drive away. We had been driving for about five minutes when little Nick suggested that we say a prayer and ask for God's help in finding the right car. He was more focused on the correct approach to our car hunting that morning than I was, and I took his suggestion as a reproach from God.

Along the way we had to pass through the small town of Fort Ann. On a corner in the middle of town was a traffic light. We slowed down as we approached it and stopped as it turned red. We saw an auto dealership on the right side of the road, but what caught our attention was the station wagon on display in the used car lot to our left.

One glance, and I knew that the brand new looking, burgundy, Grand Marquis station wagon was way out of our price range. I wasn't even going to check it out, and when the light changed, I almost drove on. Nick, with the simple faith of child, insisted that we stop and inquire about it.

"That's the one," he insisted with confidence. "That's the car God wants us to have!"

To appease my son, I pulled into the lot, and we got out of the car to inspect the station wagon. It was in such excellent condition, at first, I thought it was a new car. We quickly learned from the salesman who approached us that the car was three years old and had seventeen thousand miles on it, just like the car Al and Maureen had bought.

I couldn't believe it. I was astounded and immediately thought that this had to be more than a coincidence. My hopeful thinking, however, was short-lived. The salesman told us the asking price was sixteen thousand five hundred dollars. I informed him that all I could afford was nine thousand dollars. While he went into the office to talk with his manager, Nick and I waited with great anticipation. Was God about to move in a miraculous way?

When the salesman returned, though, the lowest price he could offer us was fourteen thousand five hundred dollars. Not a bad offer, but I just couldn't afford it.

Needless to say, we were disappointed, but I encouraged Nick, as well as myself, that we would find what we were looking for in God's good timing. We drove on to Glens Falls and spent the whole day visiting every car dealership in the city. There was absolutely nothing available anywhere near what I could afford. As we drove out of the city north on route 22 toward Fort Ann, I was feeling a little beaten down. It had been a long, discouraging day.

Little Nick, however, was still upbeat. He insisted that we should stop and ask about the Mercury Grand Marquis one more time. I did stop at the dealership in Fort Ann just to make him happy. To tell the truth, I was embarrassed to ask about the price of the car again. I knew what kind of a reaction I would get. I had no real hope in my mind of getting that car.

THE STATIONWAGON IS OURS

We pulled into the dealership a half hour before closing time. The same salesman met us, and I restated my offer of nine thousand dollars. He shook his head in dismay, but said he would speak to his manager again. This time the manager returned with the salesman and gave us a song and dance about the value of the car and how he needed to make a profit on it. I remained firm in my resolve not to spend above what I could afford.

Both the manager and the salesman went back into the office to talk, exasperated by my stubbornness. They returned shortly and, in a not to pleasant tone of voice, the manager offered me a deal. He said that if I immediately signed the papers to purchase the car before they closed for the day, I could have it for nine thousand and two hundred dollars!

Through the insistence of my son, a child whose faith was stronger than my own, a discouraging day was miraculously transformed by the hand of God.

Just as He had done for Al and Maureen, God directed us

to a three year-old station wagon with seventeen thousand miles on it for nine thousand two hundred dollars. The car was immaculate. It had been a one-owner car. The owner had been an older man who drove it infrequently, and the original factory wrapping had never been removed form the back seat. In every way, shape, and form, it appeared to be a brand new car!

NOT A COINCIDENCE

Once again, this is not the end of the story. If it were, someone might shout, "coincidence!" Five years later, however, when we were in need of a second station wagon, the Lord answered our prayers again and led us to a three year-old, burgundy, Chevrolet, eight passenger wagon with seventeen thousand five hundred miles on it. This time we paid nine thousand, five hundred dollars. I attribute the slight increase in miles and price to inflation, but miraculous just the same. Is this still coincidence? I don't think so, because every time we were subsequently in need of another car, the Lord heard our prayers and provided us with incredible deals.

The year before my wife and I retired was replete with blessings and miracles. One of these miracles again pertained to a car. The car we were driving at that time had high miles on it, and I did not want to drive it to our retirement home in Florida. Since buying cars is my department more so than my wife's, I began to pray for another car.

COULDN'T HAVE GOTTEN A BETTER DEAL

Because of all the time we had spent in Florida over the years, I was aware that "good buys" could be found there on large luxury style cars. Therefore, I not only prayed, I began reading on-line the newspaper from North Port, Florida, where our new house had been built. It was in early March of 2004, after three or four months of praying and watching the newspaper ads when I saw an advertisement in the want ads that mentally blew me away. I wasn't sure if what I found was from the Lord, but I began to get that special feeling one gets when God starts orchestrating events in one's life.

What had caught my attention was an ad for a three year-old Crown Victoria, four-door sedan with one thousand five hundred miles on it. I though the ad must be in error, and the car probably had fifteen thousand miles on it. At the right price this car would fall into the pattern of blessings God had been bestowing on us over the years.

I called about the ad and learned the seller was a gentleman in his eighties who had fallen ill shortly after purchasing the Crown Victoria. He hadn't been able to drive it much, but he hung on to the car for three years hoping that his health would improve to the point where he could drive again. When this did not occur, he moved into an assisted living facility and placed the car up for sale.

He explained that he had paid close to $29,000 for the car and had been asking $18,000 for it. Now, after three months of not being able to sell the car, he offered it to me for $11,500. Not exactly the three year-old $9,000 scenario, but this was years later, and the ad had given the correct mileage. This car only had one thousand five hundred miles on it.

Of course, human nature as it is after the fall of Adam, I was leery of the deal and not yet ready to proclaim another miraculous blessing. I wished to check it out further. I continued to pray about the car, and I also called my son Nick who had returned from the mission field. He and my daughter-in-law, Wendy, were living in our new house in Florida as caretakers until we retired. Nick contacted the seller on my behalf and learned that the old gentleman resided only several minutes from our Florida residence.

Nick went to see the car and within a half hour he called me back. "Dad," he said, "get your checkbook ready. This deal is for real! The Crown Victoria actually has 1,480 miles on it. It is loaded with options, has leather seats, and is in, mint condition!"

Have you ever heard the expression, "You couldn't have gotten a better deal if you had a gun in your hand?" Well, this was the case, except I didn't need a gun. I had a Heavenly Father looking out for my best interest. All I had to do was pray, trust in Him, and respond to His promptings. At the time of this writing, my middle son is driving that Crown Vic as a second car. It has 130,000 miles on it, and it has not needed any major mechanical repairs.

STILL ANOTHER MIRACLE CAR

After four years of retirement and living on a fixed

income, the value of which seemed to shrink by the week as all living expenses shot skyward, my wife and I looked at our latest "miracle" car and realized that we had driven it many miles. We were ready for another car but, because of limited finances, we had to be frugal. Of course, we knew that God would intervene according to his own timetable and provide for us as He had done in the past. I don't even recall saying more than a few passing prayers concerning a new car. We simply trusted in the Lord. We were confident in His continued provision.

Once again, the Lord did provide. The miracle of the cars continued for us in another unexpected way. We had been including an elderly woman friend by the name of Cathy in all of our activities and holiday gatherings since our move to Florida. She was a close friend of both my mother and my aunt. Cathy was almost ninety-two, living in an assisted living facility, and still driving. No sooner had we started thinking about the need for another car, than Cathy mentioned to us that she should turn in her license and sell her car.

"I'm just not as alert as I used to be," she would say, "and I'm getting a little bit forgetful."

This was definitely an understatement of her mental condition and driving ability. To give you an example, after dinner at our home one evening, I walked her to her car with an umbrella, and ran back to the house to escape the heavy rain. I watched her car roll down my driveway across the street and stop perpendicular to it. As soon as I realized there was a problem, I ran down to her car. By this time it was really pouring, and I could not hear what she was yelling to me through the closed car door.

Cathy tried to roll her window down, but it didn't seem to be working. Finally, she opened the door and told me that the car just died on her. The fact of the matter is that she never started the car to begin with. She merely turned the key part way and placed the gearshift into neutral which allowed her to roll down the driveway. I simply reached in and turned on the ignition and told her to put the car in drive.

Away she drove into the rainy night on an angel's wing and my prayer.

The idea of buying Cathy's car was in my mind, but I gave it little thought. It seemed as if Cathy would continue to drive forever, and a sales price was never mentioned. Eventually, Cathy did stop driving but held on to her car just in case she needed it. It was almost another full year before she died at the age of ninety-three, and it was only a couple of weeks before her passing when she decided to sell the car to me.

Her car was a 2001 Crown Victoria, the same year as the one I currently owed. The difference was that it had been driven less than fifteen thousand miles. She only wanted four thousand dollars for it, which was less than half of its true value. Cathy became ill and passed away suddenly without consummating the deal. However, she had expressed her intentions to her son who was the executor of her estate, and he honored the sale after her death.

I passed on my old Crown Vic with ninety-six thousand miles to my son, and I replaced it for four thousand dollars with another Crown Victoria of the same age with only

14,800 miles on it. Once again, God's blessing was truly bountiful. There is absolutely no doubt in my mind that over the years we have experienced a string of miracles that served a very practical purpose for us. At the writing of this book, we are still driving Cathy's car. Furthermore, I am confident that when the time comes for another car, God while provide another amazing deal for us.

DEVOTION TO GOD'S WORK IS FURTHER BLESSED

The miracle of the cars was even more far-reaching, as it over-flowed into our need for a second vehicle, a pickup truck. Back in 1999, we were considering retirement, and we viewed our financial situation in a new light. Over the years we had not accumulated much in the way of savings nor made investments in preparation for retirement. Instead, we had devoted ourselves to the various ministries to which God had called us, trusting that when the time came for us to retire, He would fulfill all of our needs. We were not worried about saving for our future. In essence, we placed our future in God's hands, trusting that we would not be disappointed.

As I prayed earnestly for God's will concerning our retirement, I discerned that I should build a house to sell for a quick profit (see the next chapter on the miracle of the house). I also started praying for a pick-up truck that I could use for that purpose and as a second vehicle for our youngest son, Nick. He was about to return home from mission service in Africa, and he had been encouraged by my wife's sister Myra and her husband Shane to pursue studies with Christ's Gospel Church in Indiana. Both Myra and Shane were ministers with Christ's Gospel Church in Kentucky and Indiana, and Nick held them in high esteem. Nick decided to follow their advice, and he needed his own means of transportation for the three months he planned to study with their church.

Once his studies were completed, he hoped to spend some time at home helping me build the investment house. As part of his schooling in community development with the University of the Nations in Hawaii, Nick had spent six months in Switzerland undergoing intensive training in construction technology. He was eager to put what he had learned to use helping me. A pickup truck would be ideal as a second vehicle. It would provide transportation for Nick while he was studying in Indiana and be of practical use for us when the time came to build the house.

The building of the house, as a financial venture to make money for our retirement, was a major undertaking for me. I had minimal savings and had to finance the purchase of the truck and the house construction materials through a mortgage credit line on my family home. I was praying for a reliable truck at the right price, but I really didn't know what the right price was.

VISION OF A RED DODGE PICKUP TRUCK

One afternoon while I was praying, an image of a red Dodge pickup truck came into my mind with a price tag of five thousand dollars. I had never owned a Dodge, and I wasn't particularly partial to the color red. Furthermore, at that particular moment, I didn't feel that it was time to run out and start looking for a truck. Yet, I knew in my heart that this image was more than wishful thinking. I believed it was a vision that had been planted in my mind by God. Therefore, I held on to it and waited patiently for His perfect timing.

A few months later, we had to travel to Niagara Falls to visit my father who had fallen ill. We left Ticonderoga after school on a Friday afternoon. By the time we made the six and a half hour drive, we arrived in Niagara Falls well after dark. Our first stop was Pine Avenue Boulevard, on the outskirts of the city where there was a string of inexpensive mom and pop motels. We rented a room, unpacked our luggage, and headed into the city to see my parents. When we returned to the motel, it was late, and the long drive had taken its toll on us. The only thing that had caught my attention about our surroundings was a Dunkin' Donuts shop within walking distance from the motel.

I mention Dunkin' Donuts, because I am an early riser. When I traveled with my wife or family, I had the habit of getting up before everyone else and going out for coffee. I not only relish my morning coffee but also the quiet, solitude of the early morning. Therefore, I always kept my eye open for a convenient place to get coffee. The next morning I tiptoed out of the motel room around 6:00 AM, careful not to awaken my wife. I crossed the parking lot and walked out to the edge of the highway on my way to the doughnut shop.

MY VISION FULFILLED

On the lot to the right of the motel was a small used car dealership. The vehicle they had selected as their "eye-catcher" was displayed on a raised platform. It was a red Dodge pickup truck! I could not believe my eyes. It was the truck in my vision. My heart leaped into my throat. Was this coincidental? I did not think so then, and I still do not. I truly believe that I was guided to that particular dealership where the answer to my prayers, the fulfillment of my vision came to pass.

Later that morning when I went to inquire about the truck, I learned that it was three years old with low mileage. The dealership was changing locations that very day and the manager was eager to sell the truck even at a reduced cost, if necessary, so that he wouldn't have to move it. Would you believe I purchased that red, Dodge pickup truck for five thousand one hundred dollars, far under market value and asking price, and exceedingly close to the amount given in my

Vision!

By the way, I had that truck for nine years without any mechanical problems until the rusty, old radiator began to leak. Nick used it those first months in Indiana and Kentucky while he was doing his studies, and later he made a trip with it for a vacation in Florida. When the time came, we used the truck as a workhorse to build my investment house. Prior to our retirement in 2004, Nick drove the truck again to Florida and had it waiting for me at our new home. We all used it for another four years following our retirement.

ANOTHER TRUCK PROVIDED

By the time my red Dodge pickup truck was twelve years old, the radiator and body were rusting out, but I was emotionally attached to it. It was like an old buddy to me, and I kept patching it up rather than giving it up. On numerous early morning occasions steam from the radiator would pour out from underneath the hood as I was driving my grandson to school. Eventually, the reality that I would have to part with my faithful friend hit me, and I began to pray for another truck.

I had recently been introduced to a website, Craig's List, and I started watching the ads for used trucks. Within a month, I saw an ad for a Ford Ranger pickup truck that was five years old and had approximately the same mileage my red Dodge had had when I first bought it. What attracted my attention was the price. It was far below any prices I had been seeing for trucks.

In all honesty, the asking price was so low in comparison to other truck ads, I was skeptical. I jumped to the conclusion that it was probably a junk or riddled with mechanical problems, and I hemmed and hawed about telephoning about it. Yet, a prompting in my mind finally caused me to inquire. I made an appointment and prayed for discernment as I drove the twenty miles to inspect it.

As soon as I saw the truck, something within me immediately said, "This is the one." Once I took it for test drive, I was even more convinced. While discussing the truck with the man's wife who was handling the sale, the Lord gave me a clear sign that the purchase was in His will. I bought it on the spot. You see, I learned that the couple selling this truck were "born again" Christians.

I learned that the only reason her husband was selling his truck, was because his employer had decided to provide him with a new company truck. Like me, he hated to part with his old buddy. I only paid $3,200 for that five year-old six cylinder Ford Ranger, an unheard of price at the time. I also learned that I was the first of several people who had called and made appointments to see that truck. Other potential buyers were waiting in line behind me. At the writing of this book, I have been driving that truck for close to six years and I have not had any mechanical problems with it.

When I consider all the little facts, I am totally convinced that God's miraculous hand has been at work over the years concerning the purchasing of our cars and trucks. My wife and I have been provided with thousands of dollars worth of vehicles at a mere fraction of their actual value. I am, of course, reminded of the scripture dealing with God's carrying for the lilies of the field (Matthew 6: 28-29). You see, God is present in our daily affairs, and His provision is tangible for those of us who place our trust in the Creator of the Universe. All things were created through him, and all things are still made possible through Him.

CHAPTER SIX

FINANCIAL BLESSINGS

NOT A PROSPERITY GOSPEL

I do not wish to give anyone the wrong idea that in the preceding chapter or in this chapter that I am giving witness to a "prosperity gospel." I am not. My wife and I have had our share of financial difficulties throughout our lives. We have lived simply, worked hard to provide for our family, and retired with minimal savings. We are not wealthy, but we have lived well, because we have trusted in the Lord's provision even when circumstances and difficulties were stretched beyond our human understanding.

While our children were young, for example, we decided that Donna's place was in the home with our children, rather than in the work force. My teacher's salary was meager in those early years, and I had to supplement my income by doing part-time general contracting with a friend and fellow teacher. Donna supplemented our income by providing daycare for the children of friends, women who needed to work full-time.

Prior to starting our family, Donna worked as a social worker and as a teacher. Only after our children were of school age, did she decide to return to work. The decision she then had to make was to work full-time as a teacher or part-time at our local nursing home as a social worker. Donna took the job as a social worker, because she felt a calling on her heart to minister to the elderly. Her position in the nursing home did not pay much, but it was the direction given to her through prayerful consideration, and it readily turned out to be God's plan for her.

Donna's gentle demeanor and spiritual conviction endeared her to the staff, the residents, and their families. Her ability to empathize with people soon developed into the role of spiritual counselor to the staff, especially the nurse's aides and lower level personal. God also blessed her with a gifted and powerful ministry to the dying. She was the one who sat through the long days and nights with terminally ill residents and their families, comforting them and praying them into God's loving arms.

The good Donna accomplished and the satisfaction she received from her position as a social worker far exceeded any monetary benefit she may have gained from a different position. Yes, we lived on less money, but we lived comfortably. In this instance we placed the Lord's work before our own needs, trusting Him to provide for us and for our future.

THE MONKS BENCH

My wife and I always prayed for discernment concerning work and finances, and we believed in the old adage that "God helps those who help themselves." During those years when our children were young, financial necessity caused us to be industrious. Another way we earned extra money was through the buying and reselling of used furniture and antiques we acquired from old-fashion country auctions and yard sales. We had little knowledge of antiques, as this story will tell, but we managed to have fun and earn some needed cash.

We ran from yard sale to yard sale and to various junk auctions in the small towns surrounding us, searching for "treasures" we could resell at a modest profit. We hadn't heard the term back then, but I guess we were what today is known as "pickers." We also found good buys on inexpensive furniture for our personal use in the home. We didn't own a truck at the time, and we must have made quite a sight with the furniture tied every which way on top of our car's roof.

The monk's bench was one of those pieces of furniture that immediately caught my eye at a yard sale. It was about four feet wide with squared off edges and made of oak covered with a black stain that allowed the grain to show through. It was plain but some how attractive, and it was sturdy.

I bought it for a whopping fifteen dollars. It had no seat,

so I cut and fitted in a piece of plywood, and my wife sewed a cushion to cover it. We placed that monk's bench in our family room and used it for several years. The kids drove their toy cars up one side and down the other. On occasion they even drew on it with crayons. By the time we decided to "redo" our family room and buy new furniture, that monk's bench had served us well.

THE BIG SALE

It was several years after we had bought the monk's bench, a Saturday in August, when we decided to hold a lawn sale. We put it out on our front lawn along with a myriad of other items we had collected over the years. I knew the monk's bench was an antique, and I decided to ask an arbitrary one hundred and twenty-five dollars for it, a fair price we thought based on comparable pieces of furniture we had sold.

I was also selling a one-ton Ford truck from our recently dissolved general - contracting business, and someone had made an appointment to look at it that same morning. The truck was a big money item, and selling it was my priority. A friend and employee of mine who had been working for us throughout his high school and college yeas was helping out with the yard sale. While I was showing the truck to the prospective buyer, my helper sold the monk's bench for the asking price of one hundred and twenty-five dollars.

I was elated because the truck sold. When I learned that the monk's bench also sold, I felt doubly blessed. As a matter of fact, the entire sale was a major success. My wife and I couldn't have been more pleased. We had made a tidy profit to help cover the expenses of redoing our family room. Little did we know that Satan had inserted his foot, once again, into the affairs of our life. We were new "born again" Christians at that time, and I guess Satan wanted to discourage us by stealing as much of our blessings as possible. Actually, if we kept track of each time this has happened, we could write a book on that subject alone.

UNEXPECTED NEWS TESTS OUR FAITH

The following day, a Sunday morning, as we were dressing for church, there was a knock at our front screen door. Standing on our front porch was a friend of ours who worked as a reporter for the local newspaper. Little did he know that he was being used as the messenger for a "power or principality unseen," but he was. He stood there in a state of embarrassed agitation. He did not know how to tell us the bad news he had just received over his wire service.

He warned us to be prepared for a shock. The buyer of the monk's bench we had sold the previous day, he informed us, was an antique dealer from a nearby town. This dealer had recognized it for what it truly was, one of only two of a kind in existence, crafted by some famous artisan whose name I cannot recall. The dealer immediately resold our monk's bench for $17,500! That was a big chunk of money back then. Apparently, the monk's bench was a major find in the antique furniture world, a story sufficient to be news worthy.

Fortunately, this event took place during one of those periods in our life when Donna and I were walking very closely to the Lord. We were involved in prayer group ministry, and the gifts of the Holy Spirit were manifest in our lives. For a quick moment, I have to admit, our reaction was a human one. Both of us were stunned and dollar signs flashed across our minds. Just as quickly, however, we were able to shrug off the bitter news and even see some humor in the situation.

After a moment or two, Donna and I actually turned towards one another and laughed aloud about it. Although we did not understand why God allowed this to happen, we were secure in our belief that He was in control of this situation, as well as everything else in our lives. The thought of "what could have been" only pricked us for a moment, and we really didn't bleed over it.

My aunt was visiting us from Florida at the time this incident occurred. Overly concerned for our well-being, she was beside herself with distress and anger. In her mind she saw us take a terrible financial loss. She insisted that this dealer had an obligation to inform us of the item's true value since he knew before hand what it was worth. She felt that we had been cheated and insisted that we hire an attorney to sue the antique dealer who had bought our monk's bench.

At the time I really didn't know if we had any legal grounds to pursue a lawsuit. After all, we were the ones who put the price on the bench and sold it. I would agree with my aunt, however, that any reputable antique dealer has an ethical obligation to be fair in his business practices and not take advantage of unsuspecting sellers. However, my wife and I were really not concerned about the money and gave no thought to suing the dealer.

We believed then, as we do now, that one reaps what he sows. The antique dealer was sowing greed while we were sowing faith in God. We were at peace with what had transpired. We had sold our truck, our lawn sale had been a success, and we had acquired the money we needed to redo our family room. We felt blessed rather than cheated.

At that moment and over the next few months, we had to explain to my aunt and uncle, as well as many other friends and associates, a spiritual principle, a truism, which became our witness to the faithfulness of God. That is, everything we own belongs to the Lord. We are only temporary custodians of all of our belongings and our monetary wealth. We enjoyed the use of the monk's bench for several years, and we even sold it at a profit. If the good Lord wanted us to have an additional blessing beyond that, He would have provided it. We did not in the least way feel any loss over the sale of the monk's bench or over the lost profit that could have been ours.

OUR FAITH IS REWARDED

Our attitude in this matter, our belief in this spiritual truth, shielded us from becoming victims of Satan's scheme. We were not injured spiritually or psychologically by the sale of the monk's bench, because we placed our trust and faith in God rather than in mammon. As a result, Satan's scheme to steal our blessings was cast down and trampled underfoot. Donna and I remained peaceful and joyful throughout this situation, and we continued to give witness to our trust in God.

Within a few short months, our witness grew in stature. An investment we had made in the stock market unexpectedly paid off, and we reaped a profit close to twenty thousand dollars. Incidentally, within the year, the newspapers reported that the antique dealer who had purchased our monk's bench had been arrested for stealing from clients. One does reap what he sows.

As far as we are concerned, all of our possessions do belong to the Lord. Certainly, there are times when dark, financial circumstances engulf us. Sure, we experience momentary weakness and our faith wavers when we are faced with a financial crisis. These are the times of testing when we turn to God and pray for the grace and faith to be like Job in the Old Testament. He remained steadfast in his faith even in the face of total loss and ruin. Today, like Job, we can continue to trust in the Lord when financial problems arise, because we have tangibly felt His divine love and experienced His miraculous provision throughout the years.

HANK'S NEED

Another miraculous story I can share with you because I was close to the individual at the time this blessing occurred concerns a wonderful Dutch-American man by the name of Henk. He was big in the "John Wayne" sense of being big and strong. He was a steel worker and welder who owned his own, one man, welding business in Ticonderoga. Henk had a perpetual smile on his face and a willingness in his heart to help anyone in need. He also had a heart for young people, and he always was available as a driver and chaperon for my youth group activities long after his own children were adults.

Henk and I spent a lot of hours driving teens to Christian music concerts and standing outside the auditoriums away from blaring music that otherwise would have made our bones rattle within us. The one thing that really sticks in my mind about Henk was he insisted that everyone greeting him or saying goodnight do so with a hug. This was especially true for the more reserved teenage guys who weren't quite sure about Christian activities.

Henk was a man's man who wanted to convey to young people, in particular, that it was manly to be kind, loving, and affectionate. The teens who didn't know Henk warmed up to him quickly, and the guys actually enjoyed being hugged by him in an exaggerated bear-like grip. He was a real father image, a role model, for teens who were fatherless or did not have a father they could respect in their lives.

Henk was the kind of friend who would drop whatever he was doing when I drove up to his house and workshop. Since Hank was also an excellent mechanic, I brought all of my auto and boat problems to him, which he immediately took care of. Whenever I stopped by to see him, he would invite me into his house and have his wife Maria put on a pot of coffee. The three of us would then socialize and discuss the issues of the day, or reminisce about a church or youth group activity in which we had participated. Henk refused to charge me for any of the work he performed for me. He always insisted that he was just paying me back for what I was doing as a prayer group leader and youth minister.

Henk was a proud man who never discussed his own financial situation with me, nor did he complain when his business slowed down and he fell on hard times. Therefore, neither I, nor any of his friends, were aware of his financial need until after it had been fulfilled, otherwise we would have gladly helped him out.

At this time, our Catholic Charismatic prayer group was functioning in a powerful way under the guidance of the Holy Spirit. Our faith was strong. All of us, including the youth to whom we ministered, were experiencing the gifts of the Holy Spirit and being blessed with many answers to prayers. This is probably why Henk, rather than turning to his friends for financial help, went directly to God.

Henk's faith in the Lord was not disappointed. God did respond, and Henk and his wife Maria shared their story, their miracle, with the rest of us one evening during our weekly prayer meeting. According to Henk, his business had dropped off, and he and Maria were in arrears on all of their bills. He had a couple of big jobs lined up, but he needed an immediate two thousand dollars to see him through his present situation. He and Maria prayed for help, and within a few days their prayer was answered in a totally unexpected and extraordinary way.

MAIL FROM GOD

On one particular afternoon, Henk was working in his shop with the massive sliding doors thrown open. He watched his wife walk down to the end of their gravel driveway to get the mail. He had watched his wife take this mail walk so many times, he didn't give the situation much thought.

When he next looked up for her, Maria was returning with an opened envelope, reading a letter in her hands. She was close enough for him to see a startled expression on her face. His first thought was that they had received bad news, and he stopped what he was doing to join her. What he found, what Maria was holding in her hand, was a letter from a former client of his and a check for exactly two thousand dollars.

Henk explained that he was on very good terms with this client who was a faith-filled Christian woman from a neighboring town. Like all Christians who love the Lord, they enjoyed sharing their faith experiences with one another. Over the years he had done work for her on several occasions, but he hadn't seen her or spoken to her in many months. She wrote in her letter that while she was praying a few days previously, she felt in her heart that Henk needed financial help, and she was moved in her spirit to give him a gift of this particular amount.

Henk and Maria were in awe of what had transpired, and they were eager to praise God and give Him thanks by making His graciousness known to the rest of us in the prayer group.

You see, the specific miracle was intended to bless and encourage Henk and Maria, but the general, inspiring, and tangible effect of the miracle was intended to strengthen the faith of all of us who heard about it. Henk and Maria's miracle was a witness to the rest of us, who, like myself, recall it many years later and are repeatedly encouraged in our faith.

HOUSE BUILDING

As I previously mentioned, I am not advocating a prosperity gospel. Accumulating wealth or its trappings has never been in my mind as a Christian. In fact, my wife and I were not even concerned about saving for our retirement years. We gave no heed to the financial advisors who declared that one should have at least a million dollars set aside for retirement, or to friends who had double incomes and double pensions and were investing wisely for their retirement.

We had lived modestly, and we planned on retiring into a modest lifestyle. Donna did not have a pension, but my teacher's pension from New York State would amount to almost the same dollar amount I had earned while working. We were content with this, and we simply trusted that when the time arrived to retire, God would provide for us as he always had done in the past.

Please understand that I am advocating complete trust in the Lord, but I am not advocating total disregard for using common sense. A person always has to discern what God would have him do to be a "good steward" of what He has provided. One must continuously pray for guidance to discern his circumstances and employ his talents wisely. To do otherwise would be pure foolishness. This is why over the years I bought and sold used items and why I was a partner in a part-time construction business. Five years before my retirement, the idea came to me while praying that I should build a house and sell it at a profit as a means of financing a retirement house in Florida.

We owned a beautiful and desirable one and a half acre parcel of land at the foot of a mountain only one mile away from our residence in Ticonderoga. Although I had never built a house, I felt that the skills I had honed doing general contracting over the years were sufficient for the task. The location of the land in itself would be a selling point for a new house, and the proximity of the property to my home would make it easy for me to come and go after school and on weekends to do the work.

PRAYERFUL DELIBERATION

The idea of building a house was an appealing one, but it was also a very scary one for me. I had no delusions about building a house. I knew from experience that it would be a monumental undertaking and, from previous encounters with "Murphy's Law," I was fully aware that it would be utterly frustrating at times. In fact, I also knew that what the secular world labeled "Murphy's Law" was really Satan biting someone whenever he could. I also knew that I would have to finance the construction of this house on credit and hope to sell it quickly.

On the positive side, it would be fun to create my own house plans and watch the work of my hands take place as the construction unfolded. Furthermore, since two of my sons would be available to help me, it would be a great family project to which we could look back on with pride. It would also be a good way for the boys to earn money through the summer. I had woven labor costs into my financial equation, and I planned on paying them.

The big question in my mind was whether this idea was just the result of my own fanciful thinking or the prompting of God. Unsure of what I should do, I started praying for guidance. I did not want to bite off more than I could chew nor move in a direction not intended as part of the Lord's plan for my future. However, for the pure pleasure of it, I started drawing up plans for my dream house while I prayed.

Everyone got into the act and offered suggestions, sometimes unwelcome ones, for improvements to my designs. At times this stressed me out and made me question further whether or not I should build a house. The upside of this is that it caused me to pray harder.

It was during this time of prayer that God led me to the purchase of my pickup truck (see section on miracle of the cars), which I would need to build the house. After eight months of praying, I felt it was time to apply for a building permit, but I remained cautious. I prayed for another month asking God to stop me from taking this step if this project was not of Him. When nothing happened to deter me, I applied for the permit and began clearing the land in the spring of that first year.

So far, I had not invested any significant amount of money in this endeavor. My youngest son, Nick, had returned from his studies with Christ Gospel Church in Indiana, and he and I were doing most of the clearing ourselves. As needed, I hired a high school boy to help out, but his salary was not a real consideration. Consequently, I still was not financially committed to this undertaking. Once again I prayed, asking God to stop me if I were not functioning in accordance with His will. After another month of prayer, for the first time, I felt as if I was doing the right thing, and I jumped in with both feet.

DESPAIR

Everything seemed right. Our oldest son, Demian, was home for the summer from studying law at Regent University, and Nick had recently completed a construction school in Switzerland as part of his studies for his degree in community development. We were ready, willing, and able!

Then the unprecedented rains began to fall. As a result, we encountered one delay after another. First, because of the mud, we could not get the bulldozer into the property to remove the tree stumps and grade the land. Once this was accomplished after falling behind schedule for two weeks, we brought in the backhoe to dig the trench for the footings, but the rains continued to fall and collapse the previous day's work. We had the same problem constructing the frames for the footings. Time and time again we would have the frames level and ready, but before we could pour cement, the rain would wash our work away.

To make a long story short, by the time the end of the summer arrived and my oldest son had to return to law school, all we had accomplished was the construction of the footings, the monolithic slab, and the framing up of the first floor of the two-story plus attic size house. Under normal weather conditions, we would have had the entire house framed up, the roof on, and the doors and windows in place.

I now gained a new insight pertaining to "Murphy's Law." It is not just a matter of what can possibly go wrong going wrong. It is a matter of the fallen nature of man and demonic influence in the world. Mankind, whether the individual recognizes it or not, is in a continuous spiritual battle that has far reaching effects in every aspect of what one does. Furthermore, the closer one tries to accomplish God's plan for his life, the more intense becomes the battle. This is the underlying force of Murphy's Law. This is why missionaries, in particular, need to be "prayed up" before heading out into the mission field.

I had tried to remain optimistic about our lack of progress throughout the summer, but Demian had returned to law school, and I knew Nick would be leaving soon for mission work in the Dominican Republic. Eventually, the reality of my predicament hit me. No, it fell on me like a ton of bricks. The school year was about to start for me as a teacher, which meant I would be relegated to building the house after school and on weekends without the assistance of my sons. With my dream house eighty-five percent unfinished, how could I possibly accomplish this building project? Why did God allow me to get into this untenable mess? The more I thought about it, the more I felt totally abandoned by God.

Of course, I had been praying for understanding and wisdom, but battle fatigue set in. Black thoughts, fear, and depression soon engulfed me. Without a doubt, there was no way I could finish this house on my own. I needed divine intervention, and I needed it desperately.

I vividly recall sitting in my easy chair one morning crying out in prayer. I was in mental anguish, worrying about what I would do once Nick left and I was back to teaching full-time. I was worrying about the future, rather than concentrating on the present, doing exactly what scripture admonishes us not to do (Matthew 6:34).

GOD RESPONDS

In spite of my weakness, my doubts, and my fears, God responded to my need in an immediate and miraculous way. After praying in desperation on this particular Saturday morning, I started out to my building site. Within a quarter mile of my house, a tall man in his fifties was standing on the side of the road. He waved me to a stop and approached my truck. He said that he noticed me driving by the other day with building materials. He then inquired if I needed help. He further informed me that he could do all phases of home construction except for heavy lifting.

I hired John on the spot and I muttered a mental prayer of thanksgiving. I explained to him what I was doing, and he told me that his half brother, Bill, was currently employed by a local contractor but was not happy with his salary. The local contractors were paying far less than what I had always paid people who worked for me, including my sons. Since I had calculated labor costs into my building budget, by the end of the day, I had two very competent employees to help me build my house.

I do not believe in coincidence. As a Christian, I believe that when one is walking in accordance with the Lord's will, He works everything out in His perfect timing. I have no doubt that my meeting with John and my subsequent hiring of Bill were due to divine intervention. Of course, I could have put an ad in the local newspaper or looked for help by word-of-mouth and found two workers, but I had not. I had prayed instead. Furthermore, John had an amazing and miraculous story to share, which clearly provides more evidence of God's involvement in my situation.

JOHN'S MIRACLE

Remember John told me that he could not do heavy lifting. Later, he explained why. He had suffered a broken neck the previous year, and he had been confined to a wheel chair as a paraplegic with a dismal prognosis. The doctors had told him he had no chance of walking again. When we met, John had been up on his feet and walking for only the previous two weeks.

During the past year while he was wheel chair bound, his brother Bill had been caring for him with the help of a visiting nurse. The nurse turned out to be a Christian woman I knew very well. She had recently led John and Bill to the Lord and laid hands on John, praying for a healing. He was not only walking, two weeks later he was standing in my path as an answer to my prayers.

I do not wish to mislead anyone concerning the nature of miracles. Just because one experiences a miracle does not mean that all of his troubles magically disappear. Life is full of trials and tribulations, due to the fallen nature of the world and mankind. A miracle may rectify an immediate problem or fulfill an urgent need. It also will strengthen the individual's faith and draw him closer to God, but it does not provide total freedom from life's problems. Scripture admonishes us to pick up our cross and follow Jesus, as life is full of problems, one following close behind another.

Building my dream house remained a monumental task that required long and sometimes frustrating hours of labor. On occasion, mistakes were made, problems arose, friction resulted between the three of us, and a variety of other intrusions interrupted our work. Yet, God's miraculous provision of placing these men in my life was sufficient for me to get my dream house built in a timely fashion. And as an added bonus, the three of us enjoyed a camaraderie that filled many of our working hours with joking and laughter. For the most part, we had a good time building that house.

A NEW DIRECTION AND BLESSING

Naturally, I continued to pray through the whole building process. When we had the house constructed to the point where all the doors and windows were in, the water line was hooked up, the electrical wiring was done, and the sheetrock was in place where it would not interfere with the plumbing, I halted all work. The idea came to me that I could sell the house unfinished at a significant profit and save myself a great deal of time and energy. Whether or not this thought was implanted in my mind by God or merely the result of rational thought, I am not sure.

Part of Donna's and my plan was to move into and enjoy the newly built house for a couple of years before we retired. After all, it was our dream house built by my own hands according to our own design. When we prayed about this, we did feel confident, however, that selling the house unfinished was the right thing to do.

Rather than dealing with a real estate agent, I placed the house up for sale on a "By Owner" web site and received instantaneous inquiries from as far away as Florida and North Carolina. The house was sold in one week and the closing was held within a month. I received the asking price and made a nice profit that enabled my wife and me to have our retirement house built in Florida. I have no doubt that my actions were guided by God, and the Lord's timing was impeccable. Houses were in demand in Ticonderoga while property and homes were still reasonably priced in southwest Florida where we intended to retire.

Moreover, the Lord continued to provide for us as we looked for property in Florida. While we were visiting our middle son who resided in North Port, Florida, we found an over-sized, corner lot and adjacent lot only ten minutes from his house. We made an exceptionally low offer of three thousand dollars per lot, and our bid was accepted. A week or so after we returned home, we received a call from our real estate agent in Florida. The owner of the property we had just purchased was willing to sell us two more adjacent lots at the same price, three thousand dollars per lot. Buying it provided us with one large, square parcel of land, extending from corner to corner on a short street.

God had blessed us again in an unexpected way. We were able to purchase an acre and a half wooded parcel of property for twelve thousand dollars. Amazingly, it was the same size as the property we had built our house on in Ticonderoga. Within a short time, we found a model for a twenty-one hundred square foot house we liked and contracted to have it built at a very reasonable price.

Ten months later, our spacious and accommodating Florida retirement home sat on a large wooded parcel of land that was conveniently located in proximity to our son's home and the shopping area of North Port. My wife and I felt truly blessed by the outcome of what started as our prayerful house-building project in Ticonderoga and culminated with our retirement home in Florida. We attribute it to God's miraculous hand at work in our life.

UNEXPECTED BLESSING

No matter how many financial blessings one receives from the Lord, human nature is such that when the circumstances of life begin to sour, when pressure from worldly affairs increase, all of us have a tendency to buckle under the negative aspects of the weight placed on our shoulders. We forget about our past blessings for the moment and focus on our present need. Everyone experiences a sense of fear or becomes depressed from time to time. It is often said by the wise that one's walk with the Lord is full of valleys as well as mountaintops.

Just around six years into our retirement, as the economy in our nation took a turn for the worse, we began to experience some financial reversals. Since we live on a fixed income, the rising cost of food and gasoline, unexpected medical and dental needs, along with the need to provide financial assistance to family members began to weigh us down psychologically.

Foolishly my wife and I began to worry in the natural about our finances, knowing full well in the spiritual that our Heavenly Father was watching over us. Every time an unexpected bill or financial need popped up, I would fret about it. I knew in my heart that my concern over our finances was foolishness, and that I was allowing the evil one to steal our peace of mind and happiness. Therefore, I began to pray for an increase in my faith. Note, that I did not pray for an increase in my wealth. I was sufficiently wise enough to understand that I was experiencing a crisis of faith, not money.

Within a two-week period, God responded to my prayers in a totally unexpected way. I received an email from my cousin in Pittsburgh whom I was planning to visit in a few weeks. He wrote that he had a small gift to present to me from his parents who were recently deceased. My aunt had died the previous November, and my uncle had passed away the following July. Upon reading this e-mail, I felt a prompting from God and knew that He was about to bless us in an unusual way.

My aunt and uncle were not wealthy people, and I had not been expecting an inheritance from them. A particular amount of money was not mentioned by my cousin in his email, yet the amount of ten thousand dollars immediately flashed in my mind. In my way of thinking, however, ten thousand dollars is not a small gift. Therefore, I was in doubt as to whether or not that figure was actually given to me by God or merely conjured up by my own imagination.

I did not mention this amount to my wife. Rather than speculate, we prayed in thanksgiving for the blessing, whatever it may be. Yet, for close to a month, every time I prayed about this gift, the same amount of money kept popping into my mind.

In October, while my wife was attending a quilting conference in West Virginia, I drove to Pittsburgh to visit my cousin Ed and his family. I was his best man at his wedding, and we have remained close over the years. It was a pleasure just to be with Ed and his family again. I was having such an enjoyable time with them, I was not even thinking about the promised "small gift."

One evening as we all sat around talking, he handed me an envelope and card. When I opened the card, I found a check for ten thousand dollars. Tears welled up in my eyes out of gratitude for the generosity of my cousin on my aunt and uncle's behalf and for the faithfulness of God.

I called my wife the next day to tell her of our good fortune. She was not surprised. She told me that she, too, had had the same amount of money in her mind since we received my cousin's e-mail. She, too, was uncertain of herself at the time to claim it as God's spoken blessing.

I consider this a miraculous answer to prayer and a tangible experience with God, not because I came into an inheritance unexpectedly. I am sure that this type of thing has happened to other people.

The miraculous resides in the way God responded to my prayer for an increase in faith. He spoke the specific amount that we were about to receive to both my wife and me. This was His tangible way of clearly reminding us that He was still in control, orchestrating the events of our lives. He answered my prayer in a totally unexpected way but in a way that strengthened both my wife and me in our faith.

CHAPTER SEVEN

DIVINE PROTECTION

NO TREPIDATION

One of the areas in my life where God truly worked miraculously over the years was the mission field. For a number of years my sons and I traveled abroad to Third World countries to do mission work, and my youngest son Nick eventually became a full-time missionary for several years. When I first started taking my boys on short-term mission trips, I felt that it was important for them to see the abject poverty under which so many people struggled to live their daily lives. I also wanted to establish within their hearts a sense of compassion and selfless giving for less fortunate people and nations, especially those who did not know Christ. I tried to teach my sons, as well as members of our youth group, the need to be Christ's hands and feet to a suffering world. As missionaries, we were more than relief workers.

We were fulfilling the "Great Commission" to go into all the world and preach the gospel (Matthew 28:16-20).

I never undertook one of these mission trips without first praying that what I was about to do was truly God's will. I was taking my sons into Third World countries were we would encounter civil unrest, crime, and disease. Herein lies the miraculous: I always traveled without fear, and in later years my wife and I willingly placed Nick's safety into the hands of God. We trusted in Him for Nick's well-being in the mission field, as he labored in places such as Indonesia, Nepal, Benin, and Niger, West Africa.

We felt secure in that whatever my sons and I would encounter, whatever dangers or illness would befall us, God would be in control. We did not allow the darkness or even the shadow of fear to intimidate us and steer us off course. Corrie tenBoom explains what we felt when she wrote, "Never be afraid to face an unknown future with a known God."

On my first mission outreach, I took my middle son Demitri to work at Stone's Hope, A **Youth With A Mission** base in the Mountains of Jamaica outside of the city of Mandeville. **Youth With A Mission** is one of the largest none denominational mission organizations in the world. Demirti was twelve at the time. The following year when my youngest son Nick was eleven, he joined us on his first trip, and the three of us did an outreach to the island nation of Grenada. Once again, we worked at an YWAM mission.

From the very beginning, I had no misgivings and felt no

fear about taking my young boys into Third World countries where we could be faced with uncertain dangers, such as hostile individuals, disease, and lack of medical care. Certainly, many individuals have faced terrible, physical hardships in the mission field, even martyrdom. Yet, I always felt that we were in God's will, and I was peaceful in my heart about what I was undertaking with my sons.

AMPLE PROVISION

God's provision was readily apparent when we began fund raising for our mission outreaches. Our hometown friends, church, and community were supportive of our missionary endeavors and gave generously. We always received sufficient funds to meet our expenses. This sign of God's provision afforded me with more than just finances. It gave me confidence that what I was undertaking was truly part of His plan for us. Once a prayerful decision was made about a particular mission outreach, I never had any doubts, concerns, or fears about where we were headed or what we were about to do. The grace of the Holy Spirit within my soul gave me the ability to function in the supernatural and to trust in Him for all provision and protection in the natural.

FLYING WITH GOD

Over the years, however, we did encounter some situations that one might consider harrowing, but they never deterred us from our mission. During our first outreach to Jamaica, for example, Demitri and I were flying from one end of the island to the other with a very young looking pilot aboard a small, older model plane from an independent Third World air service. The propeller plane had two engines and seated twelve to fourteen people.

Midway, one of the engines began to sputter. The pilot announced that we were going to make an emergency landing in a nearby field. Needless to say, most passengers became concerned, and what began as murmuring quickly turned into loud expressions of fear. I said a silent prayer and felt the peace of God engulf me. I knew that whatever happened, Demitri and I were in His hands. I felt no real anxiety, and Demitri later told me that he was not frightened either.

The pilot made a bumpy landing without incident, and after he asked all passengers to disembark, the situation became more interesting. He told us that a mechanic was coming out to repair the engine, and we would resume our flight shortly. Whether or not the pilot had landed in this field before and knew a mechanic in the vicinity, heaven only knows.

Within a few minutes, however, an elderly Jamaican man riding on an old-fashion, red farm tractor came to our assistance. He dismounted the tractor, reached into a pocket of his greasy coveralls, and pulled out an enormous size wrench. He proceeded to walk around the plane three or four times, and on the last circuit pounded several times with great enthusiasm on the outside casing of the malfunctioning engine.

The pilot then turned to the passengers and announced that the engine was fixed. A wave of disbelief and horror flowed over my fellow passengers. All of them refused to get back on that plane. I turned to my son and asked him if he, too, was afraid to continue on. He just smiled and shrugged his shoulders. I still felt peaceful and unafraid, so we embarked, leaving the other passengers stranded in the field.

I never did find out what arrangements they were able to make. The pilot never offered any further assistance to these left behind passengers. He simply boarded the aircraft, started both engines, and flew away with Demitri and me. The other passengers must have thought that I was absolutely crazy and that I was placing my son in unnecessary peril. The difference between them and me was that I felt God's protection at that moment, while they felt only their fear. As a result of my faith, I was functioning in the supernatural while they were stranded in the natural.

ANOTHER FLIGHT WITH GOD

Several years later, after my youngest son Nick had earned a degree in community development from **YWAM's University of the Nations** and was working as a missionary to the Dominican Republic, he and I had an unusual and potentially disastrous experience while flying. Nick had come home for a visit, and I returned with him to meet the young Dominican girl, Wendy, who would later become my daughter-in-law. We flew out of Sarasota, Florida, on a plane operated by **Agape Flights**, which at that time serviced missions in the Dominican Republic and Haiti by delivering passengers, cargo, and mail.

As a nonprofit organization offering inexpensive flights for missionaries, passengers were expected to help. Nick and I arrived at the Agape hanger at 3:00 A.M. to help load the cargo and push the plane out of the hanger onto the tarmac. Unfortunately, the plane's engines would not start. We had to push the plane back into the hanger, so that its batteries could be charged. At this point, others may have had misgivings about this flight, but, once again, I felt peaceful.

An hour later, after pushing the plane back out on the runway for a second time, we flew out of Sarasota with no further problems. This flight was one of the most beautiful, breath-taking trips I have ever made. Since it was a small plane, we flew low over the various island groups on our way to our first stop at Cap-Haitien, Haiti. The panoramic view of turquoise waters and tropical islands surrounded by visible reefs was awe inspiring and relaxing for Nick and me. As we approached the northern coast of Haiti, I can vividly recall the spectacular view of the Citadel Laferriere, the mountain fortress built over a period of fifteen years by 20,000 workers between 1805 and 1820. I can still recall these majestic views and how I reveled in and marveled at God's creation.

Our pilot, on the other hand, as we later learned, did not feel as relaxed as we did. Due to the minor problem with the plane's batteries, we had fallen behind schedule by over an hour. Our retired pilot was an older gentleman, who was flying as a volunteer for **Agape**. His plans included making a return flight to Florida that same day from our second destination, the Dominican Republic. Although we were unaware of his state-of-mind, he was quite anxious about making up lost time. This became evident to us when we landed in Cape Haitien. Our pilot jumped out of the plane and swung open the cargo doors with great haste. He then began running around and shouting orders for us to get the plane unloaded as quickly as possible.

AN INJURED PILOT

As we worked, he continuously ran back and forth from one side of the plane to the other to make sure we were unloading the correct cargo and mail. In his state of agitation and impatience, inevitably he blundered. He did not duck down low enough as he ran beneath one of the plane's wings. He collided with it so hard, he was knocked off his feet and his forehead was split opened. He sat on the ground dazed and bleeding profusely from the gash on his head.

Nick responded quickly and pulled a clean T-shirt from one of his travel bags. By this time, the pilot was covered in blood. Using Nick's shirt for compression, we placed it on his head trying to stem the bleeding, but the blood continued to flow. Someone suggested that he be taken to a local clinic to have the wound sutured, but the pilot adamantly refused, sighting the lack of sanitation and the high risk of infection in Haiti. He said he rather chance flying to the Dominican Republic where he had more confidence in the medical care. We could not persuade him otherwise.

We had the plane unloaded and were ready to depart in another ten minutes, but we were not sure the pilot was in any condition to fly. Since his co-pilot was a young fellow who was only in the process of acquiring his license, we suggested that we delay the flight for a while. Our pilot, however, was adamant. He insisted that he was okay to fly. In the meantime, Nick had to provide him with a second T-shirt to absorb the flow of blood. Our pilot held the folded shirt in place over the gash on his head with his headphones as he climbed into the cockpit.

GOD AS OUR COPILOT

As we taxied in preparation for takeoff, Nick turned to me and asked what we would do if the pilot had a concussion and suffered the effects of it while we were in the air. I had already prayed silently about the situation and, once again, was engulfed in the peace of God. I told Nick that we were in the Lord's hands and not to worry. Still a little bit concerned, Nick asked the young copilot if he could fly the plane should there be a need.

I'm not sure what was going on in his mind, but our copilot paused uncertain for a moment and told us he could fly the plane, but he wasn't too sure if he could land it! Others may have been frightened by this comment, but I felt no fear. Rather, I felt the miraculous presence of the Lord. Our trust in God was rewarded with a safe journey and landing in the Dominican Republic. Our senior citizen pilot did take the time to have his wound stitched up at a local clinic, and we later heard that he had flown the plane back to Florida that same day!

PLACING NICK IN GOD'S HANDS

My youngest son Nick was the one most touched by our mission outreaches and, as he stepped out in the Lord's will, we not only prayed for him continuously, we prayed for our own wisdom to make right decisions concerning his future in the Lord's service. As parents, we were cognizant from his first experience in the mission field at the age of eleven that Nick felt a real calling in his heart. By the time he was sixteen, he had decided that he needed more independence, and he suggested that we allow him to go abroad into the mission field without me. My wife and I discussed this and felt confident that Nick was abiding in God's will. After some research and a lot of prayer, we were directed to **Teen World Outreach**, an amazing mission organization out of Lima, New York.

This mission organization sends teams of teenagers to a dozen or more Third World nations every summer. At the sending off ceremony we attended that year, they acknowledged that these teams may be heading into tumultuous situations. Typically, they ventured into parts of the world where living conditions are harsh, disease is prevalent, and medical aid is limited, not the type of places one normally would send his teenage son or daughter. Of course, I am not talking about sending someone off on a vacation.

Through **Teen World Outreach** Nick went to Nepal with a team of about twenty young people. Nick had just completed his sophomore year in high school before he left for Nepal. His team hiked the Himalaya Mountains and handed out spiritual tracks to villagers in remote areas. The people in some of these villagers had never seen Caucasians before. You can imagine what an experience Nick would have missed if we had been too protective of him and not allowed him to go. The impact of this particular outreach on Nick formulated his future plans for serving God.

Since we published news releases, and I did presentations about our mission experiences, the entire community, as well as family, friends, and colleagues, was aware of illnesses and problems we had encountered on previous outreaches. A stomach virus, for example, had incapacitated Nick and me for almost two weeks after working at **New Missions** in Haiti. On numerous occasions individuals approached me with concerns about safety and health issues. They asked how my wife and I could be so unconcerned about Nick's welfare.

The truth of the matter is that we were very concerned. We were concerned enough to employ the most powerful safeguard we had at our disposal, prayer. We prayed for Nick continuously and placed him into the hands of a loving God, our Heavenly Father, who had a plan and a purpose for Nick's life. As the lyrics of an old spiritual hymn state, "... no fear, no dread... I'm leaning on the everlasting arms of His love."

Some people had a difficult time accepting this explanation. They were more accustomed to viewing all circumstances from a worldly perspective in which doubts and fears have a tendency to dominate one's thoughts. They hadn't grown sufficiently in their faith to step out of the natural into the supernatural realm where one can feel the tangible touch of God and walk in the freedom of His light, rather than in the fear inducing darkness of the natural world.

We were functioning on a higher spiritual level, and the assurances we received from God were not just nice thoughts but real, tangible, miraculous touches of grace that filled us with confidence and a peace that surpasses all understanding according to the world's standards.

A GIANT STEP FOR THE LORD

Nick returned from Nepal more "on fire" for the Lord than ever before, and he was eager to return to the mission field as quickly as possible. In fact, he had worked out a plan to present to his mother and me. He asked if it was possible for him to double up on his high school classes and complete his junior and senior academic requirements in one year rather than two. He wanted to utilize what would have been his senior year in school to travel to Africa aboard a medical missionary ship.

Nick had researched his idea of working as a volunteer support staffer aboard the **M/V Anastasis,** which is Greek for the Resurrection. Now a retired vessel, at that time, it was the flagship for **Mercy Ships**, a medical missionary organization founded in 1978. This organization operated the largest non-government hospital ship in the world.

My wife and I had no qualms about Nick's plan to take this next step as a missionary in the service of God. We first had encountered **Mercy Ships** and its youthful volunteers in New Orleans while attending **The World Congress on The Holy Spirit and World Evangelization** in 1987. We were much impressed by what we saw and learned, and we immediately began supporting this ministry. We were confident that Nick's idea was a blessed one even before we began to pray about it.

Nick's academic standing strongly favored his plan to double up on his high school course work. He had been an honor student during his first two years of high school, and he had been inducted into the National Honor Society at the end of his sophomore year. He also was an excellent athlete and a highly disciplined person capable of taking on such a demanding scholastic workload.

Furthermore, I was in the perfect roll to assist him with his studies. I was an English teacher in our high school, and I had been tutoring students after school in a variety of subject areas. However, Nick's plan to "step out for the Lord" turned out to be a giant step for all of us, involving much more than we had anticipated. Whenever one steps out in faith, especially in the mission field, Satan immediately takes a stand against him, and he finds himself involved in spiritual combat (Ephesians 6:12).

FACING A MAJOR OBSTACLE

We immediately encountered a major obstacle we had not foreseen. Since my work as a youth minister and our mission service was well known and supported by the community, we had assumed that the school administration would be cooperative in such a noble, spiritual endeavor on Nick's part. Over the years, the school board and superintendent of schools had supported my Christian youth group activities. Despite the prevailing secular winds of change sweeping our nation, for many years, I had been allowed free use of the classrooms and gymnasium for my activities and special events, and I was even lauded for what I was doing.

The newly hired principal of our high school at the time, unfortunately, was not a Christian, and he had another agenda in mind. I had, in fact, bumped heads with him on a number of occasions over issues of "separation of church and state." From the beginning of this principal's tenure, he tried to thwart my activities in little ways without overtly showing his bias. Aware of the support I had from the community and school administration, he did this subtly by cloaking his actions and decisions against my activities under the guise of doing what was best for "all" students and protecting the school from becoming embroiled in legal issues.

There was some merit to his stance, since this took place during that time when the ACLU was pressing school districts to secularize everything they did, such as changing Christmas vacation to Winter Break and removing traditional Christmas carols from school concerts. Fortunately, I was able to counter his efforts against my undertakings with information provided through the Christian legal organization, **The Center For Law and Justice** out of **Regent University** in Virginia where my oldest son was attending law school.

When Nick and I approached this principal with Nick's plan to double up his course work, he adamantly refused. Using worldly logic, he argued that this would set a bad precedent for the high school. Once he allowed one student to graduate early, he hypothesized, other bright and capable students would desire to do likewise. This would open a floodgate for students who would want to complete their high school education early. It would cause, he claimed, a drain-off of the school's highest achievers and be detrimental to the student body as a whole. Certainly, this could be argued from two different perspectives.

Personally, as a professional educator, I felt that it was the school's mandate to assist each student in becoming all he was capable of becoming, especially if accelerating his education served his best interest. Unfortunately, the principal was able to sway the superintendent to his point-of-view. Keep in mind that our school district received state funding based on its enrollment. The fear of a possible loss of state funding may have played a significant roll in the decision that was made.

QUITE A DILEMMA

We were faced with quite a dilemma. As an employee of the school district and as an a teacher who advocated formal education, I knew that the decision I had to make would go against the conventional grain and not be a popular one with the school board. It also raised questions in my own mind with which I had to struggle. My decision was to "home school" Nick. Home schooling at that time was not a popular concept. It was just beginning to take root as an alternative to public education. Furthermore, as an employee of the district and as a public school teacher espousing home schooling, I would be viewed as a traitor to public education. Nick's spiritual vocation, however, was our main concern. Therefore, my wife and I prayerfully decided to take Nick out of the public school system and home school him.

There was only one Christian woman in our small community at that time who was home schooling her children based on her religious principles, and she had aroused the ire of many people in and out of the school system. She was viewed buy most as a "nut case" and frequently spoken about with derision among my fellow faculty members at the high school. I knew this woman well. Do you recall the Christian nurse who cared for and prayed over John who helped me build my house? It was she.

I knew she was sincere in her faith, and that her biblically based rationale was justifiable. Yet, I was not sure whether this approach to completing Nick's high school education would be in his best interest. Even today, I am not convinced that home schooling is for everyone who finds fault with public education. There are many, many factors that need to be considered.

PLACING NICK'S FUTURE IN THE HANDS OF GOD

One of the issues that played on my mind was the fact that Nick would not receive a diploma recognized by the State of New York nor by many colleges. I assumed that he would desire to continue on with his higher education after his service with **Mercy Ships**. I was concerned that my decision would later hinder his college opportunities and ultimately his financial security.

Another issue was athletics. Nick was a star player on the basketball team, but he would be ineligible as a homeschooler to play. My wife and I earnestly discussed our concerns with Nick. He had no misgivings. He was willing to forego his high school basketball career and to place his educational and financial future in the hands of God.

Again, after prayerful consideration and some basic research, my concerns were put to rest, and we decided to home school Nick. I learned, for instance, that Nick's S.A.T. scores and his unusual personal experience and dedication would be more significant factors for acceptance into college than the nature of his diploma.

Our venture into home schooling under the direction of our Lord was a successful one. Nick applied himself to his studies for four hours from eight to noon every day, and I assisted him whenever needed during the evening. In this manner, he completed two years of course work by the end of March of the following year, using texts and study materials through the **Abeka** program of **Pensacola Christian College.** He also took the **Standard Achievement Test** and scored well enough to be considered for college scholarships. He even won a scholarship from **Houghton Christian College**, the one traditional college to which he applied.

By the time Nick was ready to pursue a college education,

however, he continued on the unconventional path designated by God. He turned down the scholarship at **Houghton** and decided to attend a non-accredited college, **The University of the Nations,** in Hawaii. Through this religious, mission centered institution, he studied and served abroad in several different countries while earning an associates degree in Community Development.

Later, he acquired a Bachelor's Degree in Theology and was ordained as a Baptist minister. As the years passed, Nick also acquired a great deal of knowledge and experience in the business world and, by the time of this writing, he had become a regional manager for **Dunkin' Donuts** with over thirty stores under his management. Today, he is a successful businessman who ministers spiritually to his employees

A SPECIAL BLESSING IN SWITZERLAND

Since Nick was ineligible to play on the high school basketball team while he was home-schooled, he turned his attention to snow boarding during that year. He headed off to the mountain slopes in Vermont much more frequently than if he had been encumbered by the high school's rigid, daily class schedule. He was sufficiently self-disciplined to set his own pace for his studies. Whenever he decided to take the day off from his studies in favor of snow boarding, he simply made up his study time the next day. His newfound love for snow boarding not only replaced his love for basketball, it developed skills that could be used when other opportunities arouse.

Later, during the course of his studies with the University of the Nations, for example, Nick learned to surf. The Lord rewarded him with the pleasure of surfing in Hawaii, Indonesia, and the Dominican Republic. He was also provided with a totally unexpected and truly special blessing. While studying construction technology in Switzerland, he became best friends with a fellow missionary student who was the Swiss National Snow Boarding Champion. In this friend's company, Nick was able to experience a dream come true, learning from the best while snowboarding in the Swiss Alps.

The blessings Nick received were not just a matter of coincidence. They were miraculous, tangible touches from God, the direct reward for turning his back on the conventional, worldly way of doing things and responding to the call on his life from God. As scripture tells us, he placed God first in his life, and all things were granted unto him (Matthew 6:33)

Once Nick completed his year of home schooling and had been accepted to serve as support staff on the M/V Anastasis, our middle son, Demitri, decided to join him. Demitri had already completed his freshman year of college, and after what we had gone through with Nick, it was no big deal for us to approve Demitri's decision to interrupt his education to serve the Lord. In fact, we were ecstatic about the boys serving together and having one another for moral and spiritual support. In our human weakness, it was easier for us, as parents, to send the two brothers off together, rather than to just trust in God to care for one son by himself.

FACING PERILS AND HARDSHIPS

But trust in God we did. The M/V Anastasis was headed for Benin, West Africa, and the boys needed an array of inoculations before they could fly to Europe and join the ship's crew. I will never forget what transpired when I drove Nick and Demitri to the county health clinic in Plattsburgh, New York. When the nurse who was giving the inoculations learned of the boy's destination, she was aghast. She directed our attention to a world map, which contained demographic information about disease. She knowledgeably pointed out that the boys would be working in a county where a variety of diseases were rampant, including malaria.

This was not news to me, but the way she presented the stark reality of the jeopardy the boys would be facing did touch a nerve. My wife and I already were fully aware that there would be other perils to face besides disease. Like all parents who love their children, we were concerned about the health and well-being of our sons. Through prayer we fortified ourselves, as we fought on the daily battlefield of our minds where Satan is a master statistician at spiritual warfare.

We either could give in to our natural doubts and fears, or we could turn our thoughts over to the Lord our God. We chose to place our trust in the Divine. In doing so, we effectively turned the lives of our sons over to His care, trusting that no matter what perils or hardships the boys encountered, they would be in God's will.

The boys returned home safely after having one of the

most profoundly gratifying experiences of their lives, but they did have to pay the price for stepping out in faith as missionaries. They encountered many different hardships, which began immediately once they left port in Holland on their way to Benin. The Anastasis sailed into a gut-wrenching storm in the North Atlantic, the worst weather conditions the ship had faced in its entire history. The ship's crew and missionary staff were so debilitated by seasickness, a special layover in the Azores was needed for rest and recuperation.

Once they arrived in Benin they faced another challenge from nature. They encountered temperatures that frequently reached over one hundred and ten degrees on the deck of the Anastasis. Their discomfort was so great, it was virtually impossible to sleep below deck and a struggle to sleep above deck because of the intense heat. Consequently, battling fatigue became a daily routine.

Our sons also faced other dangers that as parents we never even thought about, such as being charged by a herd of elephants. This actually happened when a team they were on stopped to observe a herd of elephants in the wild. They foolishly left their Land Rover and walked closer to the herd to take photos. Fortunately, like the parents who hear for the first time from their grown children about the perils experienced in their youth, we only heard stories like this after the boys had returned home safely.

One situation that did test our faith as parents was learning that Demitri had contracted malaria. One might think that our first reaction would be to cry out, "Why have you failed us, Lord?" but it was not. Our life experiences while walking with Jesus over the previous years taught us that we are not exempt from suffering or even disaster. We had encountered, struggled through, and survived many storms. What we learned was to pick up our cross, follow Jesus, and trust in His Divine Providence.

This is what we did. We prayed, "Lord, heal Demitri in accordance with your will." We were willing to accept the outcome, whatever it would be, just as I had been willing to accept the outcome when I dropped my hand on the table saw several years previously. We were not disappointed by placing our trust in God. Our prayers were answered. The doctors aboard the Anastasis immediately diagnosed Demitri's malaria and treated him effectively. By the time he returned to the States, he was cured, and he has not suffered any relapses or ill effects over the subsequent years. The quickness with which he was healed, I believe, once again, touches on the miraculous. It certainly has strengthened our faith and given us reason to praise God.

UNDER AN UMBRELLA OF PROTECTION

As Nick continued on the path to study and become a full-time missionary, we were given further cause to prayerfully place him into the hands of a God in whom we had learned to depend on and trust. I wish I could put into words the sense of peace we felt about Nick living and serving God under an umbrella of supernatural protection. Nick was only nineteen when we saw him off on a second trip to West Africa, to Niger where he would train under the auspices of **World Vision** as part of his college course work. This time he was traveling alone, and he had to make several different plane changes in places where he did not understand the language as he hop-scotched across the Dark Continent. He readily admitted this was a nerve-racking experience for him.

A MILITARY COUP

When Nick had been in Niger for only a couple of months, we were given a serious cause for alarm. We learned that a military coup had taken place. We got the news on a Friday afternoon from friends who had heard about it on television. The president of Niger and some top ranking generals had been assassinated. All public communication in Niger, telephone, radio, and television, had been seized and closed down. This was before everyone had access to cell phones and laptop computers. Due to the communications blackout, we had no means of learning any more details about what had transpired or how foreigners were being treated. We literally had no way of contacting Nick.

If there is cause for parents to worry, this volatile and dangerous military coup was it. To say that my wife and I were not anxious, would be a lie. We were not seized by panic as some people would have been, but we immediately turned to God, seeking Divine Intervention for Nick and peace of mind for ourselves. As we prayed for Nick's safety, our anxiety dissipated. We felt the peace of the Lord flow over us just as it had on many previous occasions.

Did we understand that missionaries who are under the protection of the Lord still have bad things befall them, that missionaries are imprisoned and even martyred for their faith? Of course we did. Yet, as we prayed over the course of that weekend, we became more curious than worrisome to learn about the details of how Nick was faring. An aura of peace surrounded us, and we were secure in our belief that God was watching over Nick.

The following Monday afternoon, we received a phone call from our son. Realizing that the international media most probably had picked up on the coup, Nick assumed that we would have heard the news and be concerned about him. He told us that he had been out on the street in the market place when the coup took place. He witnessed the military vehicles rolling through the streets and the soldiers setting up roadblocks and guard stations on major intersections. Nick was not stopped or molested in any way as he traversed the streets on his way back to **World Vision** headquarters. He told us that in the course of the weekend, a new president was placed in power, and the country had returned to normal.

Apparently, the old president of Niger was not well liked by the citizenry, and the coup was not resisted or even questioned much by anyone. Through this event the pervasiveness of evil in the mind of man was illustrated for us. A few days later we read on line an account of the coup in an English language newspaper from Niger. The new government released a statement to the public concerning the former president's demise. The official declaration from the new government was that the old president had experienced an "official accident." Only corrupt men blinded to truth and morality could contrive such an euphemism for assassination and expect the world to accept it.

FACING A WORLD GRIPPED BY EVIL

From a biblical perspective, the Third World is what it is, because these nations are in the grip of evil, which manifests itself through self-aggrandizement, greed, the lack of respect for human life, and violence. Back in the early nineties while working at **New Missions** in Haiti, for example, we heard horrendous accounts of how people were intentionally run down by drivers of large work trucks. The roads were in terrible condition. Rather than driving in a straight line down one side of the road or the other, vehicles had to zigzag along the highways to circumvent huge potholes.

Keep in mind the fact that Haiti is the poorest country in the Western Hemisphere, and nothing much in the way of improvements have taken place. In fact, due to the 7.0 magnitude earthquake at the beginning of January 2010, conditions have worsened. Throngs of homeless people live along the edge of the roads, and the roadways are congested with walkers both day and night. Neither the disrepair of the roads nor the large number of people walking on the roadside seemed to be a deterrent for speed or lack of caution by truck drivers. Back then, if people got in the way, they were simply run down without a thought.

Incredible as this may sound, just before we arrived at the mission, a local teen was run over by one of the work trucks. The driver did not stop. Family members took the boy to a hospital in Port-au-Prince. The staff left him on the hospital floor untreated where he eventually died. He was refused any kind of medical care until someone from the mission would sign documents agreeing to pay the medical bills. By the time the family was able to contact the mission and have someone come in person to the hospital, the boy died from lack of care.

Where evil is prevalent, human life is devalued and danger lurks around every corner for the individual. That summer we served with **New Missions** in Haiti, we only traveled in convoy with United Nations forces for protection. In Jamaica we encountered guards at our hotel with shotguns or machine guns for our protection from thieves. Likewise, in the Dominican Republic we encountered guard towers in the parking lots of the supermarkets and witnessed guards open fire on a shoplifter as he ran away. Even when we went out for dinner and parked our car in the lot at a restaurant, we were greeted by a guard with a shotgun who escorted us inside. This is the reality of the Third World where human life is cheap.

Disease is another constant factor faced by missionaries who venture into the Third World nations. On one particular outreach to **New Missions** in Haiti, despite all the precautions we took, Nick and I became violently ill. And we were not the only ones. Well over one hundred adult leaders and teens who were participating in a special outreach at this time were infected. Everyone had returned stateside two days before Nick and I were scheduled to leave, and some people were so sick, they had to be taken off their flights by stretcher.

Word of everyone's illness had quickly gotten back to us that next afternoon. Nick and I, as yet, had not become ill. I began to pray that we would be spared, and we went to bed early that evening feeling okay. We had to catch an early morning flight out of Port-au-Prince to St. Croix in the U.S. Virgin Islands, as we had plans to work at a **YWAM** mission there.

We were not spared, however. In the middle of the night, I was awakened by Nick moaning in his sleep. When I checked on him and put my hand to his forehead, I found that he was burning up with a fever. There wasn't much I could do but pray. By the time we reached St. Croix, both of us were violently ill, and the good folks at that mission had to care for us. We were ill for at least ten days. Why did God allow this to happen to so many people. Well, if there were a hundred of us who became ill during that outreach, there probably were at least a hundred different reasons. I am sure, however, that all of us, including the caregivers, grew spiritually as a result of our illness.

The truth is that we are fragile creatures susceptible to disease and mishaps. Furthermore, from the moment we are born we begin a progression toward death. Simply stated, we need God in our lives. We need His grace to handle life's situations, and we need Him to help us carry our burdens. Illness and mishaps remind us of how frail and vulnerable we truly are. They can be spiritual growth experiences if we turn them over to the Lord. They also help to prepare us for the moment of our own demise when we must turn our very existence over to God.

I mention these things concerning the Third World to illustrate the evil conditions missionaries typically face in their efforts to bring Christ to a hurting world. The fact that my sons and I, like thousands of other missionaries, were able to face these conditions without debilitating fear is part of the miracle of faith. If we had attempted to work in the mission fields of the Third World on our own accord, we would have been defeated by our own human frailty and fear for self-preservation. Only by walking on a path illuminated by Jesus Christ, The Light of the World (Psalm 119:105), and turning ourselves completely over to our God were we able to feel His touch and receive his protection while serving Him. For us, functioning in the supernatural realm, where there is little room for doubt or fear, is a real miracle.

CONTINUED GUIDANCE AFTER MISSIONS

Several years later, after Nick and Wendy were married in the Dominican Republic, they decided to leave the mission field and return to the States. God continued to guide their lives and provided them with clear and purposeful direction. It was just before Thanksgiving of that particular year of their return, when Nick and Wendy came to Ticonderoga to stay with us and make plans for a future career. My wife and I had not retired, as yet, but the construction of our house in Florida had been completed that previous October.

Since Nick and Wendy had been running a missions program for inner city children in the Dominican Republic for the previous three years, they were considering a career in teaching. The problem, of course, was that neither of them had stateside certification as teachers.

Nick and Wendy had given this some thought, and they

had sought out the Lord's direction in prayer. They formulated a sensible plan for Nick to apply for a teaching position at a Christian school where his mission experience working with children would be viewed as a plus on his resume, and where the requirement for a teaching certificate would be less stringent. Wendy was still learning to speak English, and she hoped to pick up a part-time job to supplement Nick's income.

Knowing that we would soon be retiring to Southwest Florida where one of his brothers and several other relatives already resided, Nick made a list of all the Christian schools in a several town radius of our retirement home. He then began contacting each and every school whether or not it had an opening for a teacher.

As he began making phone calls and sending out resumes, Nick found that several Christian schools would not even consider hiring someone who was not a certified teacher. He also found that salaries for Christian schoolteachers were considerably lower than their counterparts in the public schools. This, however, was not a deterrent for Nick and Wendy. As missionaries, they possessed little and were accustomed to living frugally. They were willing to make sacrifices as they developed their future, one step at a time.

Furthermore, our retirement house was sitting unused, and it was equipped with basic furniture and housewares. It would be available for their use as long as they needed it, and it would eliminate the monthly expense of renting a house or apartment. Most importantly, however, for Nick and Wendy was their assurance that God had a plan for them.

God's provision for their future arrived quickly in a most unusual way that, once again, touched on the miraculous. One of the schools to which Nick had sent his application was operated in conjunction with a small Baptist church in Englewood, Florida, about a twenty-minute drive from our retirement home.

The principal of this school was a young, former businessman by the name of Robert. At the request of his pastor, he had recently walked away from the business world and stepped into his new position as financial director and school principal where his business acumen was needed to turn around this financially troubled church and school. Robert, in fact, was reviewing applicants to fill a position in his school when he received Nick's resume.

Robert had not felt comfortable with any of the applicants he currently had under consideration. Yet, the moment he read Nick's resume, he felt God tell him that Nick was the one to hire. Following a telephone interview with Nick, Robert hired him sight unseen. After Christmas Nick and Wendy moved to Florida where a whole new life began for them. In addition to teaching classes, Nick was appointed the director of the church's afterschool program and summer program. This of course was an additional financial blessing for him. Wendy was also hired as a substitute teacher and an assistant in the afterschool and summer programs. The additional program salaries enabled Nick and Wendy to meet the needs of their growing family and to live comfortably.

As time passed, Robert and Nick became "best friends." Both of them were ordained as ministers and functioned as assistant pastors at that church. Robert became a mentor to Nick, and the financial acumen and management skills that Nick possesses today as a "director of operations" for a company that owns Dunkin' Donuts and other fast food franchises were acquired under Robert's auspices. In spite of the unusual educational path Nick had followed, his future success was not hampered, because his career was and still is being orchestrated by God.

CHAPTER EIGHT

UNEXPECTEDLY USED BY GOD

DECEPTIVE DIRECTION

Would you believe that God knows what He is doing? Long before I had my "born again" experience," God was molding me and forming me for my work as a youth minister, and I had no idea of what was taking place. In college I had majored in English, because it was my weakest discipline. I was a high school dropout who had earned a high school equivalency diploma while I was in the Marine Corps. This diploma was my ticket into our local community college, but it had not provided me with much in the way of language skills.

I wisely surmised that whatever occupation I pursued in life, a written and spoken command of the language would be a plus. I had never given any thought at all to teaching, however. I merely assumed that a liberal arts degree would open doors for me in whatever occupation I decided to pursue.

My wife Donna graduated from college two years before me, and she immediately started working as a social worker with **Catholic Charities**. She had majored in sociology and knew exactly what she wanted to do. On the other hand, when I graduated in 1968, I didn't have a clue about what profession I should follow.

I did have a fondness for the tropics and a desire to return to the Caribbean where I had been stationed with the 2nd Marines Expeditionary Unit. The first year we were married, Donna and I vacationed in Puerto Rico. I knew the island well from my Marine Corps days, and we had a wonderful time enjoying the flavor of the tropics. Donna was always agreeable to a little adventure, and with this in mind, I came up with a plan for our future.

MY PLAN OR GOD'S PLAN

We only had been married two years and had no savings to speak of when I graduated from college. I suggested that I use the funds we did have to fly to Puerto Rico and look for a job. My rational was simple. If I traveled by myself, we would not only save on airfare, I could keep my expenses down by staying in a cheap, back alley hotel off the Condado strip in San Juan, the type of place to which I wouldn't dare expose my wife. Once I found a job, Donna could follow. Note how self-assured I was. The idea that I might not find a job never even occurred to me.

One benefit of serving in the Marine Corps was that the experience developed in me a confidence and bravado sometimes carried to the extreme of cockiness. I had no fear of staying in a seedy area of San Juan were rooms were cheap. I selected a hotel a few blocks away from the elegant Condado Beach Hotel. The room was old and basic and had a sign prominently posted on the wall that said, "Don't Drink the Water."

The proximity of my hotel to the Condado Beach Hotel was the reason why I chose this particular establishment. Every afternoon after job-hunting, I donned my swimsuit and flip-flops, threw a towel over my shoulder, walked the couple of blocks to the Condado Beach Hotel, and boldly strolled through the lobby as if I were a guest there. I then would use the hotel beach and pool area at my leisure.

A DIVINE APPOINTMENT

The first time I tried this ruse, I encountered a minor problem I had to circumvent. The swimming pool and beach were fenced, and a matronly woman in her sixties was checking the guests' room keys at the gate. Thinking fast, I did not allow this to deter me. I casually approached this woman while she was watching the ebb and flow of guests and struck up a conversation with her. I found her to be quite friendly and eager to talk about herself and her life in Puerto Rico.

After about ten minutes or so, I commented that it had

been nice talking with her and that I hoped to speak with her again. Then, unhampered, I simply walked into the "guests only" area.

I did the same thing on the second day, and by the third day this friendly gatekeeper waved to me when she saw me approaching. I had endeared myself to her and had become a friend who had no need to show a room key. Moreover, I actually enjoyed talking with this woman. Speaking with her took the edge off the loneliness I was feeling from being separated from my wife. I tell you this story about my nefarious behavior to relate to you how God will redirect our actions toward the purpose He has planned for us in spite of our personal detours and sinfulness.

After four days of unsuccessful job-hunting, I was beginning to get discouraged. I learned that salaries in Puerto Rico, even for brass, young college graduates, were low. On my fourth day's excursion to the Condado Beach Hotel, I confided my job dilemma to my new friend who had impressed me as being a wise and knowledgeable person. She asked me if I would consider teaching and told me that the Department of Education in the US Virgin Islands was desperate for teachers. Furthermore, it was only a half hour flight to get there and the fare was a mere fifteen dollars each way.

Following her advice, I flew to the US Virgin Islands the next day and boldly walked into the Department of Education without calling for an appointment. I was welcomed with opened arms and immediately ushered into the office of the personnel director. As soon as the director realized I was married, she inquired as to whether my wife would like to teach. In a matter of a half hour, I was able to secure teaching positions for both my wife and myself with benefits that included a relocation allotment.

Who would have thought that my bold trespassing at the Condado Beach Hotel would lead to a teaching career for me that lasted thirty-six years. I found that I was a natural born teacher. My gift for gab and my light-hearted joking manner gave me an edge when dealing with young people. I also enjoyed working with my students outside of the classroom where I could get to know them on a more personal level. Over the years I was an advisor for various extra-curricular activities and a tutor. Later, my metamorphosis into a youth ministry and youth conference speaker was a natural progression for me.

Little did I know that my job-seeking trip to Puerto Rico was being orchestrated by God toward a greater end. When I used the boldness I developed from my Marine Corps days to crash the swimming pool and beach area at the Condado Beach Hotel, I had no idea that a divine appointment had been made for me with a matronly woman whose advice would change my life forever. While I was enjoying my deception and chuckling over how clever I was, God was directing me along a path that would lead me into Kingdom Work.

YOUTH GROUP CALLED FORTH

As I mentioned previously, once I attended my first

charismatic prayer group meeting and had my "born again" experience, my life changed dramatically. I now began to function in accordance with the promptings of the Holy Spirit. The Lord knew that as a teacher, I was a capable and confident speaker, whether dealing with young people or adults. In a very short time, He called upon me to put my talents to use in "Kingdom Work." In a matter of a few short months, I gradually took over the role as prayer group leader, and Donna and I immediately began reaching out to our circle of friends and to our church.

As our prayer group increased in size and I began to develop a youth ministry, our efforts were greeted with mixed reactions, some being excessively negative. The Catholic Church, as a whole, did not embrace the Catholic Charismatic Renewal. In many small town parishes, such as my own in Ticonderoga, the renewal was outright rejected by the clergy. At times homilies were actually preached against it and against my personal involvement with it. We not only faced criticism but outrage. Ridiculous rumors quickly developed over innocuous incidents that were blown out of proportion.

A CULT

One evening, for example, a close friend by the name of Jim Wells and I ran a program for teens in the high school gym. Jim was associated with an organization called the **Fellowship of Christian Athletes** and had a true heart for evangelizing young people. Our presentation that evening was a teaching about God as our Heavenly Father. As part of our illustration, we turned off the lights in the auditorium so that it was pitch black. We asked the teens to picture God in their minds. While the lights were out, aides set up a tall stepladder in the middle of the gym floor. Jim sat atop it dressed in a flowing white robe with white hair and beard, depicting the traditional concept of God the Father's heavenly appearance. It was merely a humorous illustration to make a valid point.

When the lights came on and everyone had a good laugh, we explained that this is not necessarily the way God actually appears. By the next morning, rumors were already circulating around town that Jim and I were trying to start a cult and asking kids to dress in white robes! Other rumors and criticisms in the days to come were much more hateful and even fell into the category of character assassination.

At one point, I was even threatened by the pastor of our church. He told me that if I did not stop working with my youth group, he would denounce me from the altar at Sunday Mass. I actually had to contact our bishop who immediately took steps to silence the pastor. By the way, this pastor basically was a good man. It is my understanding that later in life, after being transferred to a new parish in which a Spirit-filled prayer group existed, he actually embraced the charismatic renewal.

The point that I wish to make is that whenever anyone attempts to do a significant work for the Lord, he will encounter the forces of hell mustered against him. The evil one will even use the weaknesses or fears of well-intended individuals for his evil purposes. However, for the individual who puts on the armor of God and remains steadfast in his work (Ephesians 6:11), tangible evidence of God's presence is soon manifested.

My first attempts to work with youth as a spiritual leader where within my own Catholic parish, but eventually I felt called to work across denominational lines in conjunction with other youth leaders in three communities. I established my own youth group, **Teens For Christ**, which flourished for close to twenty years. In later years, both my son Nick and I were called upon as conference speakers for youth rallies of varying denominations in our area. I was even blessed to be the guest speaker on a couple of occasions for our local Christian Women's group, which financially supported my work with the youth.

AN UNKNOWN PRIEST AND HIS PROBLEM

Our adult prayer group started out small but grew gradually in size and stature. Word of our spiritual efforts spread throughout a three-town radius, and we soon gained a reputations for being good Christian folks rather than kooks. Consequently, the most profound and far-reaching example of how God moved through the efforts of our prayer group and the "calling" He had placed on me occurred within that first year of our new spiritual life.

Since the priests in my own parish were not open to the renewal, we had to organize our own religious services. Periodically, we held a charismatic Mass in our home celebrated by Msgr. Noel Zimmerman, a wonderful, charismatic priest from our diocese who was always available to assist us in our spiritual efforts. Typically we would host between a dozen to twenty people in our home for a Mass.

On one particular evening, as we were setting up for the Mass, there was a knock at our front door. When I opened the door, I found a priest unknown to me entreating entrance. He said that he had heard a charismatic Mass was going to be celebrated in my home, and he wished to participate. He further explained that he recently had been assigned as the parish priest in Crown Point, the next town north of Ticonderoga. He was an elderly priest by the name of Father DeRoche. We were delighted to have him with us, and he concelebrated Mass with Msgr. Zimmerman.

Later in the evening, Fr. DeRoche took me aside to explain a problem he had and to ask for the prayer group's assistance. He was an old-fashioned priest with little knowledge of the Catholic Charismatic Renewal. However, having heard good things about the renewal and our prayer group, he turned to us for assistance. He explained that when he was reassigned to Crown Point, he encountered a tragic and spiritually devastating situation affecting several of his parishioners, all members of the same family.

During a family gathering, a house fire broke out and five members of this family perished. Three of them were children. This tragedy had shaken the faith of the family to its very core. The family could not understand how God could allow such a catastrophic event to befall them. They could not be consoled, and one father who had lost two children in the fire, I later learned, was on the verge of committing suicide.

Fr. DeRoche was a loving man dedicated to his calling as a priest. He had been praying and earnestly seeking for a means of helping this distraught family. Even though the Catholic Charismatic Renewal was alien to him, he had heard good reports about our prayer group, and he was moved to investigate us as a possible source of spiritual assistance.

That evening was Fr. DeRoche's first encounter with the renewal. As he witnessed the holiness and sincerity expressed by the way we worshipped during the Mass, he knew that God was at work in a special way through our prayer group. When he took me aside privately toward the end of the evening, Fr. DeRoche asked if I would come to his parish and give a presentation about the charismatic renewal with the intention of starting another prayer group. He said he would do everything possible to convince this distraught family to attend that introductory meeting.

SPIRITUAL TRANSFORMATION

I agreed to speak, but not without anxiety. I was relatively new at being a prayer group leader, and I hadn't as yet been bolstered in my faith by experiencing the countless miracles that were yet to come. At my bequest, the prayer group prayed for God's guidance, and I specifically prayed for courage and wisdom.

God provided me with sufficient wisdom to immediately realize that I could not console this family in the face of their horrific loss, nor could I say anything convincing about how God works in mysterious ways. Neither I nor anyone else possessed the ability to turn their sorrow into gladness. I prayed, therefore, that I would have the fortitude to be obedient, to go to this parish, and allow the Holy Spirit to touch hearts through what I was led to say.

God had been at work through Fr. DeRoche, and a path had been laid out in advance for me. He had convinced this entire family to come to my first presentation. I kept it simple. I spoke about my own background. I testified to my own "born again" experience and how God was pouring out His Spirit across the world through the Catholic Charismatic Renewal. I simply told this family that if they gave God a chance, He would make His presence known to them and comfort them in their suffering.

If you think about this, you will see that I made a relatively bold proclamation. In essence, I assured the members of this family that God would become a tangible entity in their lives. Yet at this point in my life, I hadn't experienced most of what I am relating to you in this book.

Whatever I said and how I said it is not the real issue. I simply stepped out in faith and made my presentation. It was the Holy Spirit who used my words to profoundly touch each member of this family and to restore this family's faith in a God, after having experienced such a heart-wrenching tragedy. This family, along with other parishioners, returned the following week, and a new prayer group, a combination of our original group and the Crown Point people quickly took root and flourished in that parish.

As the weeks passed the gifts of the Holy Spirit (1 Corinthians 12:1-11) flowed, and everyone experienced signs and wonders, the tangible proof of God's presence with us. As we laid hands on and prayed over one another, miraculous psychological and spiritual healings took place. The Holy Spirit fell afresh on us as individuals and as a prayer group, drawing us into a greater awareness and awe of our Lord and Savior, Jesus Christ.

This family not only found peace and joy in God despite its tragic loss, it became the mainstay of the parish. Furthermore, this family was instrumental in assisting me with the development of my first youth group. All of us became close-nit friends, and their children were members of that first youth group. This extended family became actively involved and assisted me as chaperons for all of our youth group activities and conferences.

Remember the father who was on the verge of committing suicide? He and his wife were with me at the charismatic youth conference when God slapped me into compliance. They were part of the team that assisted me as I prayed over young people during that healing service. As the years passed, this extended family also continued to financially support the mission work we undertook.

From unbearable sorrow, to joy, to service, this extended family was lead by a loving Heavenly Father who tangibly touched individual lives. All that I had to do, initially, was to allow myself to be used of God, and all they had to do was open the doors to their hearts when Jesus knocked.

The amazing thing to remember about this story is the immediate change that occurred in this family after my first, brief presentation in their parish. This family, burdened with sorrow and suffering beyond comprehension, was not comforted by me. This family was not touched by me. I could not possibly have changed their individual hearts in unison.

Each individual family member was touched instantly by God. A miracle took place. They experienced God in such a tangible way that each one was convinced of His presence and His reassuring love for their family. I and the other prayer team members who, likewise, stepped forth in faith to help, were merely instruments used by God.

GRACE SAVES MY AUNT

The Bible tells us that a prophet in his own land is not accepted (John 4:44). This scripture refers to the fact that Jesus' message was not heard by his own people, the chosen people of God. Like all profound statements in Holy Scripture, it presents a truth that possesses a far-reaching implication for all of mankind. Anyone who has tried to witness about Jesus to unbelieving members of his own family or close friends can give testify to the validity of this scripture. It is generally easier to witness to a stranger than to a family member or friend.

During those early years following my "born again" experience, I felt obligated to witness to my own relatives. At the time I had one aunt in particular who presented a real challenge to me. She was my Aunt Natalie, my mother's youngest sister and a woman with whom I was very close since my childhood. As a young career woman, she was the one who bought me those extra special gifts, such as my first new suit, took me on memorable vacations horseback riding, and drove me to the train station when I enlisted in the Marine Corps. She was vivacious, athletic and knowledgeable. I looked up to her and cherished her advice and friendship.

Even after Donna and I were married, Aunt Natalie visited us during the summers on a regular basis, and we always looked forward to her visits. Following her divorce from her first husband, she met and was living with a wonderful man, a Jewish businessman, whom we had accepted as family and referred to as Uncle Leo. My aunt had been raised Catholic and married her first husband in the Catholic Church. She was not a practicing Catholic, but because of her spiritual upbringing, she felt God tugging at her heart. She wanted to be legitimately joined together in marriage with Leo in the eyes of the church.

Aunt Natalie started attending church, explored her options, and upon the advice of a friend who was a Catholic priest, went through the cumbersome and tedious process of having her first marriage annulled. Even though Leo was Jewish, he loved Natalie so much, he agreed to her wishes. Once the annulment was granted and the path open for marriage, she and Leo asked me to be their best man at their wedding.

By the time my own spiritual walk with the Lord had

matured, Leo and Natalie had become very wealthy operating their own business. Unfortunately, success changed my aunt. She had become a heavy drinker, and her demeanor had become bossy, arrogant and snobbish. Whenever we were together, my attempts to discuss spiritual matters with her were always met with derision and belligerence. She just did not want to hear what I had to say.

Mammon had become Aunt Natalie's idol, and she had no need of God. Prestige and wealth were her main concerns in life. Her vision had become obscured by the world, and she could not fathom what I meant when I tried to explain to her the concept of being "born again" or having a close relationship with Jesus. During her last visit to see us in Ticonderoga, she exploded with anger in a restaurant during our dinner, She yelled at me, "Christian! Christian! What the hell is all this Christian crap you're trying to sell me!" That was how my attempts to evangelize her ended, or so I thought.

Once again, however, the Lord called on me in an unexpected way. Shortly after her return to her retirement home in Florida, Aunt Natalie learned that she had cancer. She and Leo kept the seriousness of her illness to themselves, even when the disease had spread throughout her body, and her prognosis had become a terminal one. My wife and I did not know how seriously ill she was until my uncle called us with the news. We heard from him toward the end of May of the following year.

During our telephone conversation, Leo cut to the quick. He said to me, "If you want to see your aunt again, you need to come to Florida as soon as possible. She doesn't have long to live."

I hastily made arrangements with the school district to take a leave-of-absence that would coincide with the Memorial Day weekend, and I booked a flight to Florida. As I made these preparations, I functioned under a haze of apprehension that clouded my mind. I was deeply concerned in my spirit about what I would say to my Aunt Natalie before she died. She needed to hear the salvation message, but I was fearful of upsetting her at this critical juncture in her life.

What could I possibly say to her that she hadn't already rejected? I did not want to have a repeat performance of the anger she so vehemently expressed the previous summer. This would be my last opportunity to speak to her about Jesus, and I absolutely dreaded the thought of doing so.

Even though I prayed for the guidance of the Holy Spirit, I felt at a loss to handle this situation. I prayed continuously during my flight to Florida, beseeching God for the wisdom and words to speak, to comfort, and to save my aunt. As distraught as I was, I could not find assurance in my prayers. As my plane flew into a darkening sky, my trust in God also seemed to diminish along with the setting sun. The boldness that I had possessed in handling other situations eluded me. I was just too emotionally involved to think straight.

I arrived at the airport in Fort Myers, Florida, a little after ten o'clock at night, and was met by my Uncle Leo. I knew that we had an hour and a half drive north to their home in Nokomis, and I felt ill at ease with him. I really didn't know how to express my own sadness or how to comfort my uncle, so I just allowed him to talk and explain what was happening from a medical perspective. I learned that Aunt Natalie hadn't been out of bed nor eaten any solid food for close to two weeks. When I heard this, I wondered if she would even be able to carry on a meaningful conversation or grasp what I would attempt to explain to her spiritually.

This thought no sooner passed through my mind when my uncle informed me that Aunt Natalie requested to be awakened as soon as I arrived, no matter the hour. She wished to speak with me immediately. His words were like a spark in my mind and soul that ignited a flame of awareness of the Holy Spirit moving in this situation.

I felt the tangible presence of my God. He touched me, and my fears and doubts fell from me. My confidence was instantaneously restored. I knew that God not only was at my side, but that He had already planned the course I would follow into my aunt's heart and soul. All I had to do, once again, was go to her and trust in the Lord to accomplish the rest.

We arrived at the house just before midnight, and my uncle went to the master bedroom to awaken my aunt. I stood in the living room waiting calmly to be ushered into her room, knowing that the miracle of her salvation already had been accomplished. I merely had to carry this miracle into my aunt's bedroom on the platter God had provided. The platter was something God had molded and shaped over the years, my ability as a teacher to explain something clearly and succinctly.

Within a few minutes, my uncle beckoned me to enter my aunt's bedroom. As I did so, he quietly glided out and closed the door to provide us with privacy. I encountered a very thin, frail figure propped up on her pillows. Aunt Natalie was a mere shadow of her former self. Yet her appearance, her coloring and the smile on her face did not give me the impression of a deathly ill woman.

There was a radiance about her, and as soon as she spoke, I discerned what it was. She took my hand as I approached her bed, smiled at me and said, "Remember what you were trying to tell me about God? Tell me again."

We, as aunt and nephew, were no longer functioning in the natural. For the next hour the words flowed effortlessly from my mouth as I presented the salvation message to her, answered her questions, and prayed with her. The glow on her face was that of a Holy Spirit inspired soul shining within her. When I finally went to bed in the wee hours of the morning, I was not only a man who had comforted another person; I was a man who had been comforted. My worries for my aunt had been dispelled. My Aunt Natalie was a saved child of God, and the threat of death no longer bore a sting (1 Corinthians 15:55).

The tangible hand of God was evident during the next couple of days. My aunt rallied that morning and got out of bed. For the first time in two weeks, she felt hungry and had a taste for pizza. For the next few days, we had a wonderful time together reminiscing and laughing over all the good times we had had and all the foolish things we had done over the years. I later learned from my uncle that once I left, Aunt

Natalie returned to bed and her health regressed to what it formerly had been. Uncle Leo also told me that my aunt was a different person after my visit. For one thing, she insisted that he pray the **Our Father** with her every evening.

Aunt Natalie remained bed ridden but lingered on longer than anyone had expected. I like to think that God was giving her some time to grow spiritually before He introduced her to the glories of Heaven. I was on a mission outreach in Jamaica with my son Demitri when I received word from my wife that Aunt Natalie had passed into the spiritual kingdom of Heaven. I mourned my loss of her but rejoiced in her gain of Heaven.

CHAPTER NINE
MORE REFLECTIONS

When you walk with the Lord and make a sincere, daily attempt to do His bidding, in spite of your past sins and personal imperfections, an unbroken link to God, a bond of goodness, prevails. Your life becomes a reflection of all that is good. You reflect Jesus who is the light of the world, and you help shape the lives of others, sometimes without even realizing what is taking place.

Oftentimes the current of life changes quickly from one moment to another while you are preoccupied with many different elements of just living. Consequently, you may not be cognizant of the spiritual force you are generating. Walking with the Lord can be like driving in a car while talking with a fellow passenger or just wandering through your own thoughts. Before you realize it, you have passed landmarks without really being aware of them, and you are further along on your journey than you expected to be.

I need to clarify what I mean by, "walking with the Lord and reflecting goodness." Very few of us possess such a saintly demeanor that we walk with the Lord continuously. Continuously means that the action continues on without pause. It never ceases. That has never been me and, most probably, not you. However, most sincere Christians walk with the Lord and reflect His goodness continually or on a frequently recurring basis. Therefore, in spite of our "bad moments," our lapses of integrity, or mood swings.... the various forms of sinfulness that flow from the weakness of our humanity... we live our life in a habitual way which reflects the fact that we are stamped with the sign of Jesus' cross. The result is that we have a positive impact on others.

In fact, by just living in a godly way and following the Lord's will in the particular station of life that has been assigned to us, we are fulfilling the great commission (Matthew 28:16-29). We are performing Kingdom Work for the Lord. Our work may not be as apparent as being a youth minister, a missionary, or church committee member, but it is still the Kingdom Work the Lord has called us to perform dutifully, and the impact we have on others just by our example can be far reaching beyond our own understanding.

Whenever I reflect upon my past and how God's presence in my life has influenced me in diverse and miraculous ways, I do not merely recall the greater, more dramatic or profound events, such as the healings or financial blessings. I also recall the more subtle ways he has used me to influence others in my life. Following are some of my reflections of how Christ-like actions affected the people with whom I came in contact and how God became a tangible presence to others through my wife and me. Of course, all of us affect others and are affected in return through our daily interactions. The question is, "What do you reflect?"

MISSING MOMMY

My wife had gone to church one Sunday morning, leaving me to care for our sick, three-year old son, Demian. I was not aware of how much he missed his mother until our telephone rang. I left little Demian in the toy room just off our living room and went into the kitchen to answer the phone. My time on the phone was brief, but I had my back turned toward the kitchen entrance. As I ended the call, I turned and saw my son standing there watching me intensely.

With a very serious expression on his face he asked me, "Was that God calling?"

At first, I wasn't sure I heard him correctly.

"Was that God calling?" he asked again.

"Why do you think that was God on the phone?" I enquired.

"To tell us that mommy could come home from church now?" he replied.

The center of little Demian's world at age three was his mother, as it rightly should be. He knew that she had gone to church to visit God, but he missed her. His little mind did not, as yet, comprehend the true nature of God or His relationship to us. Yet, it was the most natural thing for him to assume that God should call our house and grant the desire of his heart. How impressionable little minds are and how amazing are the connections they make with the limited knowledge and understanding they possess.

My son was expressing the simple faith of a child. Young children, who are raised by loving and nurturing parents, have the faith to simply believe that they will receive what they need when they need it. Through our love and reflection of God's goodness, my wife and I instilled this faith in our son in such away that his expectations extended beyond the natural.

Without any great theological thought, Demian knew there was a God, and he believed God would send his mommy back home to him. As parents and grandparents, it is our sacred duty to reflect the light of God to our children. This is Kingdom Work. We may not see specific results everyday, but the end result will be the gradually shifting of our children's focus from mommy and daddy to our Heavenly Father as the center of their existence.

SCARED

Our grandson Jack was four and a half years old when I took him and his seven year old brother Nick for a hike in the woods. It was a cool, overcast January afternoon in North Port, Florida. We pulled into the deserted parking lot at a local forest preserve with which the boys were unfamiliar. When we got out of the car, we encountered a dark and foreboding sky. The denseness of the forest and the widespread, reaching limbs of tall oak trees overgrown with hanging moss created an eerie scene for the two, little, not so intrepid hikers.

The boys looked around with concerned expressions on their faces. Jack was the first to speak. He uttered one hushed but emphatic word, "Spooky!"

His older brother Nick asked him with false bravado, "You aren't afraid, are you?"

Jack replied without a moment's hesitation, "Yes, I'm afraid. And Jesus is here with me, and He's scared too!"

Even little Nick saw the humor in his brother's statement, and we both got a good laugh out of it.

Of course, Jack's comment provided an opportunity for me to explain again something that Jack had previously been taught. That is, Jesus was, in fact, with us, and for that very reason, we had nothing to fear.

I find it interesting that Jack's first fearful thought was really a call for reassurance that Jesus was with us. He responded this way because other people in his life had reflected Jesus to him.

For a youngster of Jack's age, fear is fear, and I don't really know the depth of his understanding in that particular circumstance. I was able to talk him out of his fear, however. We continued on our way, and we had an enjoyable hike that afternoon. As a grandfather, I simply talked to my grandsons from the perspective I held in my heart. Without delving into great detail, I passed on to Jack and Nick the idea that we can place our trust in a God who watches over us.

Reflecting upon this situation a little further, I know that on many occasions throughout my life when I encountered dark woods and gnarled undergrowth, the Lord has fortified me with memories of other people who have reflected His light to me, especially during my formative years.

I recall Sunday mornings in the spring and summer when, as a child, it was a common sight for my neighbors to be walking past my home on their way to church. I can envision my grandmother sitting in her living room reading her Bible. I can recall my mother's insistence that I go to church every Sunday. I can feel the presence of my Uncle Richard sitting next to me eating breakfast in the basement of my Catholic elementary school after having sponsored me for my Confirmation. Countless people in all walks of life, whether they were aware of it or not, have performed Kingdom Work and greatly influenced me.

HEAVY METAL (STRYPER)

Back in the late eighties I was well established in my youth ministry work. As a high school teacher, I encountered dedicated Christian youth who functioned solely within the parameters of their individual churches and youth groups. More often than not, they had little or no spiritual interaction with other youth outside their own church activities. I came to know who these kids were, and I felt a calling to create a youth organization that would bring them together as much as possible. Like-minded Christian kids needed peer reinforcement as much as anyone else. I also saw these kids as a potential witness to other unreached students.

Therefore, I developed **Teens For Christ**, a nondenominational youth ministry, and I used my popularity as a teacher to draw my students into it. My efforts were well received by the school, the community, and most of the churches. Donations from individuals and successful fundraising activities made it possible for me to provide a wide variety of activities and events for the young people. These included basketball and volleyball nights during the week, as well as on weekends, Christian music concerts in nearby cities, weekend youth rallies, and a four day campout at the Creation Music Festival in Pennsylvania, to name a few.

We were involved in so many activities that, at times, I felt worn out, and I would falter in my desire to do what the Lord called me to do. On one particular occasion during a dreary and cold week in February, I was approached by three of my students who had never participated in any of my ministry events. They wanted to attend a Christian "heavy metal" concert at a church in Burlington, Vermont, an hour and a half drive away. I don't even know how to define heavy metal music to you but, at the time, I can tell you that I found no enjoyment in it.

The typical kids in my group were into Amy Grant, Michael W. Smith, and mainstream Christian bands. I considered heavy metal strident, raucous and grating. I had no plans to take my youth group to this concert. Furthermore, when I was approached by these three students, my first reaction was not only negative, it smacked of a prejudice that teachers some times unwittingly lean toward. These kids were students with bad attitudes who were living on the fringe of our community. At that moment I simply did not have any desire to take them anywhere, let alone to a heavy metal concert!

God's Spirit within me quickly chastised me. I checked my response and rather than just saying no, I told these kids to give me a day to think about it. It didn't take much prayer or thought for me to feel the pangs of guilt. Working with the "good kids" in my youth group was enjoyable and easy to do. My heart told me, however, that the dysfunctional kids had a greater need to be reached than the good kids. I knew what I had to do, but I proceeded reluctantly. I agreed to take them to the concert, but I wrestled with myself over this decision all week.

As the Friday night of the concert grew closer, I dreaded going even more. To make matters worse, I had caught a cold, the weather had turned bitter cold, and snow was in the forecast.

By the end of the school day that Friday afternoon, every excuse to cancel out on these kids had played through my mind a dozen times. I was ill, the weather was too bad, these kids could go with us to a different concert, etcetera, etcetera. Once again, the grace of the Holy Spirit kept the weakness of my flesh in check. I grudgingly started out for the concert earlier than usual because of the forecast of snow, and during the long drive to Burlington, I repeatedly questioned myself as to whether or not I was doing the right thing.

As it turned out, the driving conditions were better than I had thought they would be, and we arrived at the church half an hour before the doors opened. It was bitter cold, well below zero, and the wind was whipping the snow around us, chilling us to the bone. Would you believe, my three youthful wards seemed unaffected. They preferred to stand out there in the frigid night, to smoke one cigarette after another under the pretense that they were first in line and would get great seats.

As I looked at their nicotine stained fingers, my thoughts not only began to rally against these kids but also against the church people inside who officiously would not open the doors until the appointed time. Shouldn't common sense have told them that we were freezing out there!

"Dear Lord," I prayed as I began to lose feeling in my nose and ear lobes, "What am I doing here? Why are you doing this to me? Are you now extracting penance from me?" All I wanted was to get warm and to have the evening over and done with.

The doors finally opened, and the kids rushed in ahead of me, as if I wasn't even with them. My ill temper, like bile, rose up within me, and I may have growled aloud as I walked into that church. However, my ill mood was immediately tempered, as I was greeted with warm smiles and endearing blessings by the church staff. A few moments later, one of my kids came back looking for me. Much to my amazement, my kids had grabbed front row center seats and even saved one for me!

I hadn't been forgotten after all, and their thoughtfulness made me feel a little better. As I began to thaw out, the sanctuary of the church impressed me with its holiness and purpose. I began to feel at ease and comfortable with being there. Due to the weather, the turnout was minimal. The audience was small and sat close together creating a homey feeling. When the band came out, one of the musicians prayed first and introduced the other members of the band. Each member shared freely and sincerely with us about his own spiritual background, as if he were talking to family and friends.

By the time the first heavy metal number was played, I didn't mind it so much. My mind as well as my heart had been touched. I found myself focusing on the truly brilliant talent exhibited by each band member and the awesome witness they presented, as they explained the motivation for the writing of each song. Furthermore, as the evening progressed, the band shifted gears to play a wide variety of contemporary Christian music, all designed for the sole purpose of worshiping and praising God and evangelizing the audience. I had a smile on my face the entire evening. I was clapping my hands and gyrating in beat with the music. I was thoroughly enjoying myself.

While driving back to Ticonderoga in the late evening, my three teenage wards fell asleep. Glancing at them in my review mirror, it was amazing how peaceful and angelic they appeared in their repose.

The snow now was falling lightly and the roads had been plowed. The easy driving gave me time to reflect on what had just transpired. I had been called upon to do Kingdom Work, to provide God's blessing to three young people who probably needed it more than most. In the weakness of my flesh, I complained almost to the point of rebelliousness and only reluctantly responded to God's will. In return an understanding and loving God used my weakness to touch three young souls. And He provided me with an incredible growth experience of my own.

Years later, I encountered one of those three young people. She was a young woman working as a nurse's aid at the local nursing home were my wife was the social worker. We were having a barbecue for the residents when she approached me and asked if I remembered her. I couldn't recall her name, but that bitter cold winter night at the heavy metal concert immediately came to mind. As she reminisced with me and thanked me for the positive influence I had in her life, remembrance of that cold, blustery night warmed my heart.

THE T-SHIRT INCIDENT

Not all young people I encountered appreciated my spiritual point-of-view or the fact that I was a youth minister. Being both a high school teacher and a youth minister in a small town meant that most of the kids in my youth group were also my students. Back in those early years, today's liberal concern over "separation of church and state" was relatively non-existent. I frequently would discuss or organize our youth group activities with students prior to or at the end of my classes within hearing of my other students. Furthermore, I encouraged my other students to join in our youth group activities, and I even put posters on the walls in the hallways and in my classroom to advertise and entice others to join us.

Although I had a good size youth group, the vast majority of the high school students never joined. The typical student simply ignored what we were about and went his way. As the world turns, alcohol abuse, partying, sexual promiscuity, etc., as always, are much more fashionable and desirable than what the youth group offered. Every year there were students who resented the fact that I preached against the immoral activities of the world. At times they openly expressed their distain and ridiculed the wholesome and spiritual activities the youth group and I, in particular, had to offer.

Early on I acquired the sobriquet, "Father Chuck." This label was meant to mock me, but in later years the Lord turned it around. Eventually, non-youth group students, who liked me as a teacher, began to use this nickname out of fondness.

One year, by the luck of the draw, or by evil contrivance, or by divine intervention (you decide), I was given a spillover, twelfth grade class consisting of all the senior misfits, both guys and girls, in the school. Many of these kids were from broken homes or problem families who had little if any moral training, no respect for decency, and no value for education.

All they wanted do was have a good time on the weekends and get out of high school as quickly and easily as possible. I did not say they wanted to graduate, because this implies the earning of a degree. The degree was meaningless to most of them. They simply wanted to be done with and out of high school.

If they came to class on a Monday morning, they would be worn out or hung-over from their weekend escapades. Rather than coming to class to learn, they were eager to rehash their deviant behavior and laugh about the trouble they had gotten into. They frequently used foul language and seemed to find a perverse pleasure in discussing their affairs openly and loudly so that I cold hear.

This troubled me, but no matter the makeup of my class, I always treated my students in the same manner. I teased and joked with them in an effort to present the subject material in an enjoyable fashion, and I gave them every possible opportunity to be successful. I was tolerant and fair, but I was also a disciplinarian who did not allow any student to get out-of-hand. I tried to be rational and reasonable during these times, and when these students responded inappropriately, I disciplined them.

Trying to instruct this class was a real challenge. I had to spend more time controlling these students than teaching them. Some of the ringleaders in the class intentionally tried to anger me by initiating conversations with me that turned into their ridiculing Christian values. The more I stood my ground, the more they resented me. One of the antics they used in an effort to upset me was to refer to me by using my well-established nickname, "Father Chuck."

Since Ticonderoga was a predominately Catholic community, these kids associated religion with Catholicism, thus this particular sobriquet. Of course they used it as a diminutive and took great delight in scrawling it in my textbooks, on the walls in my classroom, in the hallways, and in the bathrooms. It was spoken under one's breath, and even shouted at me anonymously from the crowd in the hallways between classes. My detractors had so much fun with this particular prank that on one occasion they even made a huge sign and taped it up on the wall in the school cafeteria just before the first lunch period started.

At times this recurring prank angered me but, for the most part, I was able to laugh it off and, depending on when the intended insult was used, I was able to deflect it by responding, "Thanks for the compliment." When these miscreants realized that they were not upsetting me to the extent they desired, they came up with a new and rather disgusting idea, the obscene T-shirt. Whether they understood or not, their next antic was so disgusting and vile, it truly had to be orchestrated by Satan.

I often spoke out against some of the truly "counter-culture" rock bands of the time that were spewing out outrageously vulgar and offensive lyrics. In an attempt to counteract the negative influence of these bands, I took my youth group to all the Christian music concerts held within a couple hours radius of our community. I also encouraged all my students to listen to this type of music and pointed out the Christian singers and bands that were already popular in mainstream music. This is what gave the malefactors the T-shirt idea.

There was at the time one particularly foul band that produced and sold a sordid T-shirt that depicted a raped woman in graphic detail. I have to assume that the shirt was an illustration of one of their songs, but I do not know for sure. What I do know is that one of my male students wore this T-shirt to my class. He was sitting in the back of the room, so I was not immediately aware of his attire. From the snickering undercurrent that was taking place around him, I eventually realized something was amiss. When I walked back to investigate, this ringleader boldly asked me if I liked his T-shirt.

I was taken aback by what I saw, and I had to struggle to control my anger over his effrontery. Rather than expressing the outrage I felt, I calmly explained that his shirt was inappropriate and he needed to turn it inside out or put on a different shirt if he had one in his locker. At first he insolently remarked that there was nothing wrong with the shirt and refused to do as I requested. When I insisted, he played what he thought was his trump card, the "freedom of expression card."

"In that case," I told him, " if you really want to wear that shirt in school, all you have to do is get permission from the principal." I then asked him to go to the main office. He boldly got up and left, loudly proclaiming to his cohorts that no one had the right to tell him what he could or could not wear.

When he arrived at the main office, the secretaries were aghast at what they saw. The principal's secretary later told me that the shirt was so offensive, it took her breath away. Needless to say, when the principal saw it and encountered the boy's audacity in refusing to remove it, he immediately suspended him for three days. This was not the end of the mischief, however. The T-shirt was passed on to another member of the group who wore it to my class the next day. He, too, was suspended, and the shirt was passed on to another malcontent. After the third bozo was sent to the office, the shirt was confiscated and parents were called in. This finally put a stop to this defiant and vile prank.

After I asked each of these students to leave my class, I did not rant against him or pontificate against the immorality represented by the shirt. I simple commented to the class that the shirt was offensive to most people and, therefore, inappropriate. Similarly, as each offender returned from his suspension, I welcomed him back with out any further comment about the incident, and I treated him the same as everyone else in the class. My kindness toward these guys in the weeks to come took the wind of defiance out of their sails.

One thing I did for them, which was standard operational procedure for me, was to allow them to retest whenever they failed one of my tests. The only caveat was that the student had to come in after school for a quick review of the material. Educationally speaking, this gave me the opportunity to sit down with these guys in a small, less formal, instructional situation. Psychologically speaking, they got to see me in a different light.

As they realized that they were actually passing my class, and that I wasn't such a "bad guy" after all, their attitude toward me changed drastically. By mid-year, I no longer had a problem with them. None of them ever joined my youth group, and I do not know how many of them I may have influenced spiritually, but I did have a positive influence on them.

In fact, a few years after that class graduated, I encountered the ringleader of the T-shirt incident. He was driving a delivery truck for one of the big supermarkets in town. When he saw me, he called out to get my attention, walked over to me, and shook my hand like we were old friends. He informed me that his younger sister would be in my ninth grade class when the school year started, and he asked if I would keep my eye on her and not let her get into any trouble in school!

I shouldn't have been amazed, but I was. Sometimes being used by God can be obscure to us. We really do not understand what is taking place or what the future result will be. We, as Christians, simply need to live our lives reflecting Jesus as consistently as possible, and allow God to handle the details.

CHAPTER TEN

RESPONDING TO GOD

SKEPTICISM

Now that you have read my personal testimony as to how God has watched over my wife and myself and guided our lives over the years, again I ask, "What do you believe?" Do you have doubts about the veracity of some of the experiences I have related to you? As I explained in the text of this book, other people certainly have.

In fact, some of my greatest skeptics have been the clergy... allow me to rephrase this... some of the greatest skeptics of God's loving hand touching the lives of individuals in miraculous ways always have been our very own religious leaders. From the time that Jesus began his public ministry to this present day, those who should know better have been the most difficult to convince that miracles occur daily across the world. After all, it was the Pharisees and Sadducees who mounted public opinion against Jesus and had him crucified.

However, if you think about it for a moment, it is the miraculous signs and wonders that gave evidence concerning the profession of Jesus to be the Son of God. Likewise, the occurrence of miracles today gives credence to the veracity of what Jesus taught and is recorded in the New Testament of the Bible. As Christians of today and of tomorrow, a belief that the miraculous hand of God is still at work in the world should be a central part of our faith.

Unfortunately, depending on the Christian denomination to which you belong, you may have been taught the theological concept of cessationism, the believe that the gifts of the Holy Spirit and the signs and wonders to which I give witness were intended for the building of the early church and have ceased to exist today. This implies that since the time of Jesus and the establishment of the church, the church has not needed to be revived and doesn't need to be revived today. We all know better. There have been many revivals and new outpourings of the Holy Spirit during the past two thousand years. All have been accompanied by miraculous signs and wonders.

Possibly, you may have encountered sincere Christian fundamentalists who are very outspoken against Marian apparitions and claim the manifestation of signs and wonders associated with her are satanic. Whenever I encounter this type of rational, I cannot help but ask, how Satan, the prince of darkness, can perform good deeds. I also think of the scripture in Mark 3:20-30 where Jesus is accused of casting out demons through the power of Satan. Jesus responds by saying a house divided against itself cannot stand. Simply stated, Satan cannot accomplish anything good.

I ask you, for example, how can millions upon millions of Christians throughout the decades have given witness to miraculous events and healings if the gifts of the Holy Spirit ceased to exist two thousand years ago? How can Marian apparitions be satanic when the key messages presented by the Mother of Jesus have always been, "Turn to my Son" and "Pray." Furthermore, how can theses apparitions be figments of the imagination when they have resulted in mass conversions to Christianity?

The problem is that well-intended people and even sincere theologians think too much. That is, they try to think out and solve the mysteries of God by relying on their intellect, rather than the often time, self-evident answers presented to the world by God. To paraphrase Paul as he addressed dissention in the church at Corinth, "human wisdom can empty the cross of Christ of its power" (1 Corinthians 1:17). Scripture further admonishes us, to "Trust in the Lord with all your heart, and do not lean on your own understanding" (*Proverbs 3:5).*

In all fairness, I need to qualify the skepticism concerning miracles and signs and wonders that abound within individual clergy and in the church as a whole. There is a good reason for skepticism concerning miracles and personal testimonies. The truth is that charlatans and overly emotional people outright lie, exaggerate, and misinterpret when it comes to spiritual matters and miraculous events.

These are people who are still caught up in the evil of the world or are still Christian "babes-in arms" who have not developed spiritual discernment. Combine this with the fact that many of the clergy have never experienced a miracle, a sign, or a wonder, and I can understand the cautious stance of the church.

I am not a skeptic, but I can be skeptical. When I hear of a miraculous event I have not personally witnessed, I begin with the basic premise that miracles abound and that the very same miraculous events depicted in the Bible recur on a daily basis today. My second premise, however, is that charlatans and misguided people also abound. It appears to me that we have more businessmen and show men among the evangelists today than we have true evangelists. Therefore, I turn to the Holy Spirit and rely upon Him for verification.

Sometimes the Holy Spirit immediately helps me to discern the truth within my heart, and sometimes He does not. Therefore, if I don't receive a specific confirmation from God, I carefully consider the source of the miracle, the specific scenario, and the impact made on the lives of those concerned. I then reserve judgment until I learn the truth.

Yes, I believe that miracles are prevalent in the world today, and I profess to have experienced them. Yet, I also know that people may be mistaken or have ulterior reasons for claiming miracles in their lives or through their ministries.

In our secular saturated world where liberal theology has gained a strong foothold, many people, even men-of-the cloth, scoff at the very idea of Satan. Remember the old comedic line, "Satan made me do it!" Well, guess what? According to scripture, this is a true statement. The Bible tells us that Satan roams the world trying to devour souls (1Peter 5:8-11), and it provides us with many examples of Jesus casting out demons.

All evil in our world flows from the influence of Satan. One of his basic and most successful strategies is to deceive and use Christians who are either weak in their faith or vulnerable to certain sins. Every time a Christian is exposed for fabricating a lie or exaggerating the truth, especially in the media, many people are pulled away from Christ by Satan.

Yes, when considering miraculous events and signs and wonders, there is good reason for skepticism, but skepticism should be used to discover rather than to denounce the truth.

Why doesn't God always instantaneously verify what we hear concerning miracles? Maybe He does. Maybe it is we who, at that particular moment in time, are not in tune with Him. Maybe God uses the situation to help us develop the gift of discernment. Maybe He allows us to pursue a path of discovery leading to greater knowledge and spiritual growth. You see, all of us are vulnerable to sin. Personally, I am still in the lifelong process of overcoming sin and drawing close to God.

GROWING CLOSE TO GOD

Where does this leave us then? How is a person to determine whether or not someone like myself is telling the truth? The answer is not a difficult one.

The truth is found in God. Seek after Him. Make every effort to get as close to Him as possible. The Holy Spirit is the font of wisdom and understanding. Attending Sunday services, prayer meetings, and Bible studies is a good way to begin. However, all of these institutionalized experiences may differ considerably in accordance with denominational doctrines and even with the holiness of each individual pastor. Also, keep in mind that church services and Bible studies are essentially communal events. One needs to be a part of them, because Jesus said, "Where two or more are gathered in my name, I am in their midst." (Matthew 18:20) Yet, one's relationship with God also needs to be personal and individual.

One needs to internalize what he hears, learns, and experiences in church services and study groups. We as individuals need to take the knowledge and wisdom we acquire, and transfer it from our mind to our heart where we can develop it into a personal relationship with Jesus. Any relationship, whether it is between people or an individual and God, is developed essentially in the same way, on a one to one basis. The more time and effort one puts into a relationship, the stronger the bond and the more personal the involvement. This is the same with God, and this why scripture tells us, "Draw close to God, and He will draw close to you" (James 4:8).

One draws close to God through a disciplined, daily prayer life and reading of the Bible. I am always amazed how people will go to church religiously every Sunday but do not pray during the week nor think about picking up the **Bible** and reading it. The **Bible** is the "Living Word of God" through which the Holy Spirit speaks wisdom into our hearts. Reading scripture is essential to spiritual maturity.

Of equal importance is prayer. It is through prayer that one communicates personally with God. Prayer takes many different forms from the prescribed, traditional prayers to more spontaneous, conversational prayers including prayers of thanksgiving and praise. Personally, I use a combination of all forms of prayer. It is not the type of prayer that matters, but the sincerity that flows from our heart and soul as we pray.

Be assured, when you pray with sincerity and conviction, God hears you. He desires to respond to your needs. Never be afraid to bring everyday issues and concerns, even what may seem to be mundane, to His attention. I never start out on a drive in my car, for example, without praying that angels surround and protect me. Likewise, I never find it to be too silly to ask God to provide me with a parking place or a good seat at an event I am attending.

God really does love us. Just as we follow the lives of our children with love and concern, so does God follow the individual lives of His children. He is our Heavenly Father. This is why Jesus instructed us to pray, "Our Father who art in Heaven…" (Matthew 6:9). As a Father, God takes great pleasure in listening to and responding to our prayers. He lovingly advises and provides for his children. Through Him, we not only receive provision and blessings, the truth about all matters is revealed to us.

THE POWER OF PRAYER

Accept as a truism that prayer, whether it is institutional or private, is the most powerful source of energy in the universe, because it directly wires us to the dynamo controlling the vastness and majesty of the universe... God! If you are a skeptic or non-believer who may question how I can make such a statement in light of the power we see in tornadoes, hurricanes, tsunamis, nuclear energy, and even the sun around which we rotate, I have a simple response:

The Creator, the Lord our God who put these forces into play, logically has to be more powerful than His creation, and this can be seen throughout the ages as He has manipulated and controlled the forces of nature. In fact, the powerful forces at work in the physical world are just a mere reflection of God's power and majesty.

Note the **New Testament** story in **Mark 4:35-40** of how Jesus calmed the sea and the wind when His disciples became frightened while crossing the Sea of Galilee. So astounded were His own disciples, they asked of one another, "What manner of man is this, that even the wind and the sea obey him?"

This particular example of the natural elements obeying Jesus' command to be calm is just a small example of the controlling power God has over nature. It actually pales when compared to what is recounted in the Biblical stories concerning the destruction of the world and its rejuvenation (Genesis 5-6), the raising of Lazarus from the dead (John 11:1-44) and, of course, Jesus' own resurrection (John 11:1-

44). The fact of the matter is that every miraculous event to which I have given witness in this book is evidence of the power of prayer.

PRAY WITHOUT CEASING

When a person is connected to God through sincere, consistent prayer, all things become possible through Him who has made all things possible. Most importantly, through, prayer the Will of God, the Grace of God, and the Wisdom of God flows to the individual. This is why in 1Thessalonians 5:17, St. Paul exhorts us to pray without ceasing. A skeptic once asked me, " Why do you have to pray so much? Is God hard of hearing, or does He have to be begged?

One reason why we pray without ceasing is not so God will hear us, but so that we will hear God. Through human weakness, we have a tendency to pray for the wrong reasons or for outcomes that are not part of God's will for our lives. Prayer brings us into unity with our Creator and thus the supernatural overcomes the natural. Through prayer God becomes tangible to his people.

Is it possible to pray "without ceasing" when our daily lives demand so much from most of us? Not in a strict sense, but you can certainly live your daily life "steeped" in prayer. You can begin and end the day with prayer. You can set aside specific times each day for Bible study and prayer. You can utter a prayer of thanksgiving every time you see, feel, or experience something that pleases you, such as the blueness of the sky, the vastness of the ocean, or a myriad of beautiful sights and people we encounter everyday.

You can offer up as a prayer or even a sacrifice each task you perform throughout the day, especially the difficult ones. You can fill your car with the sound of Christian music and sing praises to God as you drive along. You can utter a prayer for protection every time you set out in your car. You can pray for God's provision for the person you see broken down along the side of the road. You can pray every time you see an ambulance speeding toward its destination or here an emergency siren off in the distance. You can pray for God's help every single time you need anything, do anything, or make any decision. I could go on and on. Without a doubt, you can saturate your day with prayer. Praying can become for you an "unceasing habit."

In case some of what I just stated seems silly or unrealistic, let me assure you that millions of Christians across the world have already developed the "unceasing habit" of prayer. These are the people who experience a tangible God in their lives and give witness to miraculous signs, wonders, and miracles. If you are not in the habit of praying and are not sure of how to pray, allow me to provide you with some situations and prayers that are part of my daily prayer life. No matter how much time I have or do not have in the morning, I begin by offering up the day to the Lord by praying:

Father, I offer up this day to You and ask to be blessed with Your unfailing love that I may sing for joy and be glad all of my days: for this is the day that the Lord has made, and I will rejoice and be glad in it. Bless my spouse, family and friends (if I have the time, I name each and everyone), and give us the grace to count this day anew that we may gain hearts of wisdom and understanding. Bless the work of our hands and our time of leisure.

I always follow this prayer by saying the "Lord's Prayer," "The Our Father," as instructed by Jesus when he was asked how to pray (Matthew 6:9-13). I am dismayed by the fact that so many evangelical and pentecostal churches avoid saying this prayer as part of their Sunday service, as it is a summary of the entire gospel of Jesus. I know what their rational is, but I do not understand it. After all The Lord's Prayer is how Jesus instructed us to pray, and it is an all-encompassing prayer.

Aware of the crazy and reckless driving prevalent in my locale, every time I get in my car I pray:

Lord Jesus, send your angles to travel before me, behind me, to my left and to my right, above and below me, forming perfect crosses of protection as I travel.

When my wife or a visitor leaves my house on a drive, I utter the same prayer for them. Likewise, whenever someone I know sets out by car on a long distance trip, I recite this prayer. Similarly, whenever I learn that someone close to me is planning a trip I pray:

Lord, reach out into the future and prepare a safe and pleasant path for them to follow. Let your travel mercies flow abundantly.

If I see someone stopped along the side of the road, and I

am unable to stop and assist them personally, I pray:

Lord, provide for them in their time of need.

If I see an ambulance or hear an emergency siren, I pray:

Lord, be there to comfort whoever is in need, and open the minds and hearts of those who will be attending them.

Throughout any given day, I frequently stop to reflect upon the goodness, the pleasure, or the beauty that surrounds me, and I utter a prayer of thanksgiving for that moment. One of my often-repeated prayers is:

Father, thank you for the goodness and relative ease of my life. Please bless those who are less fortunate.

The most important prayer that has become a mantra for me is:

Forgive me for my weakness and sinfulness. I need you, Lord.

I do not pray overtly and make a show of what I am doing. Jesus warned us not to do this (Matthew 6:6). One of my most intense prayer times is when I am swimming. I try to swim a consecutive mile two or three times a week. I find this a perfect time to focus on God and pray without being interrupted.

By nature, I am a private person. I close myself off in the prayer closet of my mind when I pray. If I am at fault in the way I pray, this is where it would be. Possibly, I am too private, and do not adequately reveal that I am a person of habitual prayer. Scripture also tells us that where two or more people are gathered in the name of Jesus, He is in their midst (Matthew 18:20). This clearly tells us that we need to avail ourselves to the power of joint prayer and public prayer.

THE SANCTIFIED PERSON

I mentioned earlier that it is the people who draw close to God who experience a tangible God. The reason for this should be obvious, but let me expound on this thought in greater depth. There is much more taking place for the individual than just experiencing signs and wonders and miracles. The person who experiences these things is close to the One who performs them. As one draws close to God and He to him, something wonderful and astounding takes place... a spiritual transformation. The person becomes sanctified. That is, through the power of the Holy Spirit residing in each person, he is set aside and made holy. He becomes an active temple of the Holy Spirit.

Does this mean that the individual no longer sins, make mistakes, or even acts stupidly at times? The answer is no. Unfortunately, all of us continue to fall short of the "Glory of God" (Romans). We continue to struggle against the snares and traps of the evil one. We continue to struggle against the weakness of our flesh.

The difference is that a sanctified person or a sanctified man, I use the terms interchangeably, understands the spiritual dichotomy that exists in the world, a division between spiritual light and the darkness of the world. All of man's thoughts, actions and activities fall on one side or the other of the division line between good and evil. The sanctified man continually strives toward overcoming all forms of evil and walking in the light of Jesus. When he slips and falls into sin, he doesn't rationalize it away. Instead he repents of his failure and is immediately cleansed of his sin through the precious Blood of the Lamb (Revelations 7:14). Most importantly, he has the guidance and the grace of God to help him overcome his sin.

The sanctified person is still a sinner, but he is a changed sinner who views his personal circumstances and the world-at-large through spiritual eyes rather than just natural eyes. The focus of his life no longer is the things of the world, but the will of God. He understands the admonishment of Jesus to "live in the world, yet not be a part of it" (Romans 12:2).

To be sanctified means to be set aside. Set aside from what? Set aside from the corruption and pervasive evil that has plagued mankind since the fall of Adam and Eve. Wait a minute. If you question this last statement, because you do not believe in Adam and Eve, if you think the creation story is just mythology, ask yourself why scripture refers to Jesus as the "New Adam" ((Rom. 5:12–21; and (1 Cor.15:20–22). Also ask yourself why Jesus died on the cross if not to overcome the fallen nature and sinfulness of man? What plan was He fulfilling and for what purpose? Believe this: The ways of the world literally are sinful and anathema to God. Sin cuts deeply. It does harm, it hurts relationships, and degrades society as a whole. The sanctified man recognizes this truth and responds appropriately to it.

The sanctified person, the changed man who has drawn close to God, is still tempted by the world, but he recognizes that the ways of the world are up-side-down and backwards. This is why Jesus said that the ways of God seem like foolishness to men (1 Corinthians 2:14-15). Men who have grown accustomed to thinking and living by secular standards cannot grasp the truth, because they are blinded to it. Truth is revealed only through the power of the Holy Spirit.

The sanctified man, the true child of God, does not need to physically remove himself from the world so as not to be a part of it. He can live in the world as long as he continuously seeks after God's will and lives according to the dictates Jesus taught us in scripture. However, the more the individual can disengage himself from living in the natural, the way the world decrees, the more tangible the spiritual realm of God becomes for him.

THE GOOD MAN AND THE SANCTIFIED MAN

I have encountered many people who simply cannot grasp an understanding of what it means to be sanctified. When I discuss spiritual matters with them, they inevitably say to me, "I'm a good person," as if this justifies the lack of any further need for spiritual growth on their part. Additionally, they fail to recognize that the term "good" is a relative one. How does one determine if he is "good?" Does he compare his values and moral conduct to what the world has to say about being good, or does he use God's standards? Possibly, it will be helpful to your understanding of what I have stated if I compare the difference between the "Good Man" and the "Sanctified Man."

The good man may be a totally secular individual, a believer in a non-Christian religion, an atheist, or a nominal Christian. He either functions wholly in the natural or more in the natural than in the spiritual. He possesses a good set of values to guide his actions, but his morals and values shift with the prevailing philosophy or theology of the times. He attempts to be self-reliant or only turns to God marginally. He strives to be successful or to do "good" in terms of the world's standards, rather than God's standards. He has a conscience, because the Spirit of God is in all men prompting them to act in a good way.

On the other hand, the sanctified man recognizes that much of what the world professes to be the right way to live and think is sinful and anathema to God. He attempts to live in the spiritual as much as possible. He may slip at times and give in to the temptations that surround him, but he weighs his decisions and actions in accordance with the morals and values delineated in scripture. He believes that he needs to be a good steward of all that he does and all that he possesses, and he relies on God for guidance. Most importantly, he places God first in his life.

The good man is kind and generous. His kindness leads him to champion causes for equal rights, because all men have the right to live life freely and pursue their own happiness. He believes that he should help his neighbor and the less fortunate masses across the face of the world. Therefore, he gives generously to charities that provide food, clothing, medicine, and shelter to the needy. When a major disaster becomes big news in the media, he is moved out of sympathy to do fundraising for the cause. He may even pray at times for the needs of others.

The sanctified man is more than kind. He adheres to the second greatest commandment, "Love thy neighbor as thy self." He has developed the habit of giving generously, both in physical assistance as well as money. He does this regularly. Most importantly, he gives not just to provide material assistance to the needy but also to "win souls" for God's Kingdom. He has, foremost in his mind, the Lord's command, the Great Commission, "Go forth into all nations and preach the Good News..." (Mark 15:16).

He also understands that all rights and freedom come from God. He "holds these truths to be self-evident, that all men are created equal, that they are endowed by their Creator with certain unalienable rights..."(U. S. Declaration of Independence). Consequently, he judges the demand for an individual's right or freedom to live or act a certain way in accordance with God's Law. He does not discriminate out of disgust, nor out of sympathy. He judges the actions of a man in accordance with God's laws, not with his emotions.

The good man will act bravely, while the sanctified man will not hesitate to lay down his life for another. The good man will ask himself if he should dedicated his time to do something charitable. The sanctified man prays, "Here I am, Lord, send me." The good man makes his own decisions about doing good deeds. The sanctified man seeks God's direction in all that he does. The good man is proud of his kindness and generosity. The sanctified man humbly accepts his responsibility to all of mankind.

Another way to understand the difference between a good man and a sanctified man is to picture an old fashion wagon wheel with the hub in the center and the spokes pointing out toward the rim. When the good man is asked to label this wheel by placing himself in the center hub and the most important aspects of his life at the end of each spoke, he may not include God in the diagram at all, or he may place Him at the end of a spoke as he has done with family, friends, education, wealth, success, etc. The sanctified man will label the spokes in a similar manner, but he will place God in the hub along with himself. He places God in the center of his life, paramount to all other aspects of his life. By doing so, the sanctified man acknowledges that God is in control of his life.

THE CHOICE

In closing, this is the point I wish to make: Too many people live wholly in the natural or more in the natural than the spiritual. They never experience or only marginally experience the supernatural, because of their self-absorption and sinfulness. They may not give any thought to God at all and pursue the affairs of their lives based on shifting, worldly precepts, or they may view themselves as industrious, kind and generous, having strived to lead a good life based on a value system, which places self-reliance, success, wealth and pleasure before God.

They may laugh at the concept of 'goodness" or believe

they are good people, because they act "good" under specific circumstance. They are either content with the status quo concerning their faith or lack of it, or they only are willing to make minor changes to draw close to God. When they do encounter the supernatural, they may grasp the reality of it for a fleeting moment, or they have every excuse and rational under the sun to discredit the experience to and turn away from it. All considered, they do not feel a real need to place God first in their lives.

Once again I ask, "What do you believe?" How did you formulate your beliefs? Are you living as a natural man or as a Sanctified Man? Do you recognize that moral goodness is based on the laws of God the Creator, and that Jesus Christ died on the cross to free mankind from the bondage of sin? Do you want to experience the tangible love of Jesus, live empowered by the Holy Spirit, and experience a tangible God who can literally transform your life? The way to do so is clearly stated in scripture: "Seek ye first the Kingdom of God and His righteousness and all things shall be added unto you" (Matthew 6:33).

A simple way to begin is to say a prayer everyday asking God to reveal Himself to you. If you are not a regular reader of the Bible, begin with the Gospel of John in the New Testament and allow God to direct your thoughts. May our Lord and Savior, Jesus Christ, bless every aspect of your life. May you and your loved ones draw close to Him where revelation, guidance, and blessing flow in abundance. May your life be guided by a tangible God.

BIOGRAPHY

Charles Serianni is a retired teacher, youth minister, and missionary. His writings are based on his experiences as an English teacher of thirty-eight years both on the high school and college levels, twenty years as the Director of **Teens For Christ**, an interdenominational youth ministry, and missionary service throughout the Caribbean and Panama. He also served as the State-side Director of **Semillas De Esperanza,** a ministry to inner-city youth in the city of Santiago, Dominican Republic.

Charles also has written a Christian novel intended for middle school age youth, **The Mystery of Docksforth's Treasure.** It is an adventure story about a family from Florida on a summer outreach to a mission in the Caribbean in the 1960's. The family becomes embroiled in mysterious circumstances surrounding the possibility of pirate treasure buried on the mission property. Woven into the plot are ghostly pirates, Obeah, 17th century ruins, caverns, and underwater scenes. Although the story focuses on two teenagers, a sixteen-year-old girl and her nineteen-year-old brother, the father who is admired by his children is a key figure. Together they solve the mystery behind the treasure and debunk the ghostly intruders. The Caribbean island, the mission, and the underwater scenes, are based on the author's personal experience living in the Caribbean, working at various missions, and many years of diving.

Charles Serianni currently lives in North Port, Florida with his wife Donna. He welcomes the comments of his readers, and he can be contacted via email: bendiga@verizon.net.

Made in the USA
Columbia, SC
09 July 2021